Disclaimer

The views expressed herein are the views of the contributors and do not necessarily reflect those of the Editors or the Tennessee Lodge of Research. Neither the Editors nor the Tennessee Lodge of Research assumes any responsibility or liabilities for the content or accuracy of any of the articles included herein. Editing of the contributed articles has included wording, spelling, grammar, punctuation, formatting, and layout.

Printed in the United States of America.
ISBN: _____

Book Design: Jason F. Hicks

TRAVELING EAST
Volume II

CHARTERED
1985

Selected Essays from the
Tennessee Lodge of Research, F & A.M.
Annual Proceedings
2006-2015

Edited by: Jason F. Hicks, J.D.

Acknowledgments

I thank the many presenters who have labored over their works like the operative masons did in the quarries. Although not every work that has been presented during the ten-year period has been selected they all made a contribution to the masonic scholarship in the fraternity. I thank my wife, Dr. Megan H. Hicks, who has patiently allowed me numerous hours to work on this project. Also, I am in a debt of gratitude to Wallace "Bush" Bernard and Mike Neulander for their assistance in this project. The formatting and citations are that of the individual authors and have not been formatted to conform.

This book is dedicated to every mason who has sought further light in masonry and I hope this book will help illuminate the way forward.

Table of Contents

Appendices

EUCLID PROBLEMATIC

By Joe Kindoll

The Forty-Seventh Problem of Euclid was an invention of our ancient friend and brother, the great Pythagoras, who, in his travels through Asia, Africa, and Europe, was initiated into the several orders of priesthood, and raised to the sublime degree of Master Mason. This wise philosopher enriched his mind with a knowledge of many arts and sciences, more especially Geometry and Masonry. He devised many geometrical problems and theorems, among the most celebrated of which was this, which, in the joy of his heart, he called Eureka, signifying, I have found it, and upon the discovery of which he is said to have sacrificed to Jehovah. It teaches Masons to be general lovers of the arts and sciences. (1)

The above, taken directly from the January 2000 edition of the Tennessee Craftsman, is certainly familiar to all men who have passed through the solemn ceremonies of our order. It has however, long been a puzzle to the serious Masonic student, by virtue of its numerous errors, questionable statements, and general lack of substance by way of any real explanation of the problem at hand.

To begin with, The Forty-Seventh Problem of Euclid states that, "In right-angled triangles the square on the side opposite the right angle equals the sum of the squares on the sides containing the right angle." Or to put it in simple mathematical terms:

$$A^2 + B^2 = C^2$$

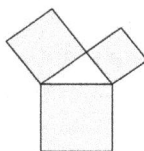

fig. 1

This well-known geometrical proof is depicted here graphically, and in form similar to that presented to the Brother during the appropriate portion of his lecture. This is, of course, familiar to anyone who studied even basic geometry in school, and is commonly known as the Pythagorean Theorem. This simple fact leads to the first significant question which the reflective Mason must ask. Why, if the world regards this as the Pythagorean Theorem, do we insist on giving it a different name? With curiosity thus aroused, other questions begin to form. Was Pythagoras in fact a Brother Master Mason as asserted? Did he actually cry out "Eureka" and make a great sacrifice? Isn't there some application of this great geometric truth more substantial than to "teach Masons to be general lovers of the arts and sciences?"

1

A fair amount is known about Pythagoras. The Greek mathematician and philosopher was born about 582 BC on the island of Samos. It is generally claimed that he spent a significant amount of time traveling throughout Egypt, Chaldea, and Asia Minor, during which he was initiated into various Mystery schools. He eventually settled in Crotona in southern Italy, where he founded a school of instruction. When his school was attacked, he fled Crotona, and died circa 500 BC. (2)

It is widely understood that the famous theorem attributed to Pythagoras was well known long before his time. Commonly referred to as "the Egyptian string trick," the practical application was to square large structures. Simply, any given length of string can be divided into twelve equal parts which are marked along the length of the string. By placing three sticks in the ground, and adjusting them so that they form a triangle, with sides equal to three, four and five marks, a right angle is formed. Thus, a perfect square angle can be created from a length of string and some measuring device, such as a twenty-four inch gauge. This application makes use of the simplest form of the right triangle - the 3-4-5 triangle, which is the form commonly depicted in Masonic circles. Pythagoras didn't invent it, but he did provide the mathematical proof, which one can presume gives him naming rights.

While Pythagoras did form a school of instruction which advanced members by degrees, to claim that he received the degree of Master Mason, is a claim too ludicrous to be taken seriously. According to Mackey, the first verifiably authentic mention of Pythagoras with respect to Freemasonry comes in a speech delivered by Sir Francis Drake to the Grand Lodge of York in 1726, in which Pythagoras, Euclid, and Archimedes are mentioned by name only as being great geometricians. Writings connecting Pythagoras to Freemasonry are, according to that author, notably absent until the middle of the 18th Century, when the new breed of speculative Masons of the 1717 revival began to connect him with the Fraternity. (3)

Nowhere in any biography of Pythagoras is the term "Eureka" used, except as published in Masonic ritual. That term is associated with Archimedes, who allegedly worked out his principle of liquid buoyancy while sitting in his bathtub, and leaping from the tub, ran naked through the streets shouting, "Eureka!" No mention is made of ritual sacrifice on the part of Archimedes, and the practice was expressly forbidden to the initiates of the Pythagorean school. (4)

This application however, is not universal, as many other jurisdictions provide no such illustration. In fact, many jurisdictions state that the lights are to be placed merely in a triangular position. Often they are arrayed in the form of an equilateral triangle BESIDE the altar, not around it.

Somewhat more obscurely, it has been pointed out that in conducting the candidate through the circumambulations during each degree, the Pythagorean triangle is formed. Indeed, during the Entered Apprentice degree, the candidate "squares" the northeast corner of the lodge three times in a clockwise fashion before changing direction. During the same portion of the ritual in the Fellow Craft degree that corner is squared four times, and five times in the Master Mason degree.5 While this is a bit more subtle and serves to illustrate some significance of the 3-4-5 triangle, it does not directly provide any deeper interpretation.

With nothing of any great substance to address these "other questions" previously stated, my attention was returned the original question concerning the naming of this proposition. What is so special about Euclid that Freemasons feel the need to refer to the Pythagorean Theorem using his name? In attempting to address this question, I decided to consult Euclid directly. Almost instantly, I found myself inundated with meaning upon deeper meaning, and a whole new perspective on the nature of the Craft.

Euclid, often referred to as the Father of Geometry, collected the sum of geometrical knowledge and understanding into thirteen volumes collectively known as The Elements. The first volume of The Elements concerns itself with planar geometry, and contains forty-eight problems or proofs. The Pythagorean Theorem is the forty-seventh, and the forty-eighth is essentially the converse of its predecessor. For all substantive purposes, the Pythagorean Theorem is the last significant proposition of Euclid's first book of The Elements. It is the Omega of that volume...so what is the Alpha?

Having found Pythagoras at the end of The Elements, I naturally turned to the beginning. To my delight, I found that the First Problem of Euclid virtually drips with Masonic application and esoteric symbolism. It essentially states that, given any finite straight line, an equilateral triangle may be constructed, using only a straight edge (i.e. a twenty-four inch gauge) and a compasses.

To begin, use a compasses to draw a circle with any given radius (Fig. 2). We have essentially created the "point within the circle" which represents each Brother. Now reverse the compasses in such a way that the other end of the radius becomes the center point, and describe a second circle overlapping the first (Fig. 3).

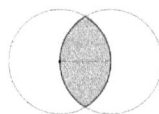

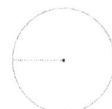

fig 2   fig 3

The resulting overlapping area is shaded in the accompanying figure. Deviating slightly from Euclid, we find in this area one of the fundamental components of sacred geometry, the Vesica Pices. This shape holds many different significations, depending upon the school of thought with views it. In pagan rites, it is held to symbolize the generative union of the male and the female. To the early Christians, it was named the Ichthys, and was displayed horizontally. The most common modern application of this can be seen displayed on rear windows and bumpers, typically with a tail attached to solidify the impression of a fish. Mathematically, the ratio of the length of the Vesica Pices to its width is 265:153. Perhaps one clue as to why this symbol came to be adopted by the early Christians can be found in John 21:11, where it clearly states that the number of fish which Jesus caused to be caught, from which he fed the masses, was 153.

Returning to Euclid, we learn that by connecting the two ends of the shared radius to either the top or bottom apex of the overlapping area, we achieve the goal of the First Problem, by creating a perfect equilateral triangle. This is illustrated in Fig. 4. But the resultant form yields much, much more than is directly given in The Elements, particularly when viewed through the lenses of sacred geometry and Freemasonry. Indeed, the equilateral triangle is almost universally accepted as a symbol of the Deity, with each side representing the principle attributes: directive, supportive, and creative, the Masonic appellations of which are Wisdom, Strength and Beauty.

Moreover the upper half of the Vesica Pices, displayed in Fig. 4 as the shaded area around the equilateral triangle, forms the exact mathematical proportions of the gothic arch. This form of arch, while different from that which is symbolically incorporated into a number of Masonic degrees, shows that the medieval operative stonemasons had a firm grasp of this application of Euclidean geometry, as this form was commonly used in churches and cathedrals of the time throughout Europe. It can still be seen to be incorporated into churches and Masonic lodges today.

The upward-pointing triangle also alludes to the male generative principle, and when combined with the correspondingly created downward-pointing equilateral triangle, a symbol of the female generative principle, the pagan interpretation is more clearly understood. The left side of Fig. 5 clearly shows these two triangles overlapped, forming a union of these two generative principles. Removing the horizontals of each (or simply not using them in the first place) yields a most familiar symbol, to Freemasons the world over.

Returning to Fig. 2, and its association to the "point within the circle," we are specifically told that the original point represents the individual Brother. In moving to Fig. 3, we are basically taking that original point, and making a single circuit around another point, returning to the place from whence we came. In doing so, we create another radius (actually two, but we can only move in one direction at a time) around which we can make another circuit. In the course of our journey through the Three Degrees, we make one purposeful circumambulation in the first degree, two in the second, and three in the third for a total of six circuits. Interestingly enough, precisely six circuits around the original center point of the first circle in Fig. 2 can be made. The resultant shape can be seen in Fig. 6, and yields a cornucopia of sacred and Masonic symbolism.

The original circle is visible in the center of this drawing, and I've kept the original radius to assist in identifying it. By adding these six overlapping circles to the original, we have created twelve small equilateral triangles. Six of them are within the original circle, and are not shown in the figure. Six are outside the circle, and when highlighted as above, clearly array themselves into the form of the six-pointed star. Within the original circle, we see that by connecting the points where each circle intersects, we create a hexagon, surrounding a central shape which brings to mind the petals of a flower. These petal shapes are almost identical to the proportions of the petals of the water lily of the Nile, and the hexagon represents the individual cell of the honeycomb, the internal (i.e. hidden, esoteric) form of the beehive.

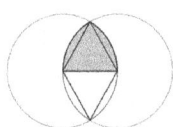

fig 4

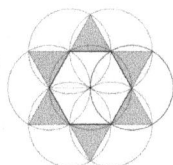

fig 6

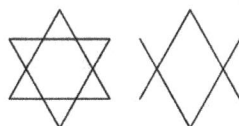

fig 5

fig 8

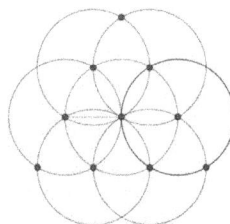

fig 7

But the Masonic application of what I have come to call "The First Problem of Euclid" does not end there. At least one other form of significance is created by making the six circuits around the original point. To illustrate this more clearly, Fig. 7, highlights several of the intersection points. The resultant form is another equilateral triangle, composed not of lines, but of points. Specifically, a triangle composed of four rows of points with one, two, three, and four points in each of the rows. This shape, more commonly referred to as the tetractys, which has so many sacred and Masonic references as to warrant an entire volume (or several) on its own.

Firstly, it is comprised of the first four numbers, which when added together, produce the sum of ten, often referred to as the perfect number. For this reason alone, the tetractys was considered to be significant, even holy in a number of the Mystery schools. In the Pythagorean school, the tetractys is composed not of points, but of ten Hebrew Yod's. In the Hebrew tradition, it is formed with four different letters, arranged as shown in Fig. 8. From this, it is easy to see how the sacred Hebrew name of Deity corresponds to that version of the tetractys. Combined with the fact that geometrically, the tetractys is made up of nine (or three times three) small equilateral triangles, the significance of "three times three" to the Royal Arch degree become readily apparent. Pike points out in his dissertation on the Master Mason degree that both Pythagoras and the Hebrew priests alike borrowed the tetractys from the ancient Egyptians. He goes on to say that it "ought to be replaced among the symbols of the Master's Degree, where it right belongs." (6)

The Hebrews in all probability learned this sacred form from Moses, who has been repeatedly identified as an initiate of the Egyptian schools, and who plays a most significant part in the symbolism of the Royal Arch degree. Pythagoras most likely learned it from the Egyptians in his reported travels there. The tetractys was arguably the greatest symbol of those who studied under him at Crotona. In fact, initiates into the Pythagorean school took their obligations, "by Him who gave our soul the tetractys, which hath the fountain and root of ever springing nature." (7) Furthermore, Pythagoras used the numerical properties of the tetractys to explain mathematically the nature of musical scales and harmonic ratios, and also the seven principle colors of the visible spectrum, emanating from the three-pointed triad of the Godhead.

So, as with many of the journeys typified in the various ceremonies of Masonic initiation, I found that I had come full circle. I began at Pythagoras, and in attempting to discover the reason behind several mistakes and odd phraseology, I found myself going through Euclid only to return to Pythagoras on a much deeper level. Perhaps, this is the exact point of all the confusing details given in the explanation to the newly made Master Mason. It exists as it is presented in order to lead us to explore and discover the deeper, hidden meanings for ourselves.

One cannot examine this very deeply without inevitably arriving at the Pythagorean Mystery school at Crotona, which has much in common with our current system of Masonic instruction. It is not however, my intention to assert that Freemasonry is descendant from this school. To do so would be just as hollow as the myriad "proofs" that our order is the direct descendant of medieval stonemasons' guilds or the Knights Templar. While both these, and other similar explanations offer interesting, and even some potentially accurate insight concerning the tangible, exoteric, or Operative origin of our institution, it is the more esoteric, or Speculative origin in which I am interested. In other words, it is far less important to prove which political organization from which we institutionally sprang than to understand the schools of thought from which we are philosophically descendant.

It is my assertion, that Freemasonry contains within it one of the last remaining vestiges of the Fig. 8 ancient system of symbolic instruction from a myriad of Mystery schools. In essence, the ancient hidden mysteries of Freemasonry are the mysteries of the Pythagoreans, the Egyptians, the Kabballists, the Zoroastrians, the Mithras, and a score of others. Our system of symbolic, allegorical instruction carries hidden within it the essence of mystic principles spanning the entire history of human existence, preserving those teachings through a modern age where such thought flies in the face of empirical and scientific reason.

Works Cited:

1) *Tennessee Craftsman, 24th Edition (Nashville: Grand Lodge of the State of Tennessee, 2000) 99.*

2) *Albert G. Mackey, Encyclopedia of Freemasonry, Vol. 2 (Chicago: The Masonic History Company, 1909) 823.*

3) *Albert G. Mackey, The History of Freemasonry (New York: Gramercy Books, 1996) 368.*

4) *Manly P. Hall, The Secret Teachings of All Ages, Readers Edition (New York: Tarcher/Penguin, 2003) 201.*

5) *Reid McInvale, "Circumambulation and Euclid's 47th Proposition," [Internet – WWW, URL], http://www.io.com/~janebm/summa.html, January, 1997.*

6) *Albert Pike, Morals and Dogma of the Ancient and Accepted Scottish Rite of Freemasonry (Charleston: Supreme Council of the Thirty-Third Degree, 1871) 88.*

7) *Hall, 202.*

THE ESOTERIC GEOMETRY OF THE TRIANGLE

By David E. Stafford, MPS (Member Philalethes Society)

This article was published in the August 2006 Issue of The Philalethes, the bi-monthly magazine of The Philalethes Society. From their website: "The sole purpose of this Research Society is to act as a clearinghouse for Masonic knowledge. It exchanges ideas, researches problems confronting Freemasonry, and passes them along to the Masonic world." (http://www. freemasonry.org)

Degree work is a pivotal part of the Masonic Lodge. Virtually every lesson taught in Masonry is imparted through the use of ritual. This mode of instruction is most impressive. Modern educators stress the importance of making the learner an active participant in the learning process. New research has also shown that in order for teachers to truly be effective, they must have a strong mastery of the skills and lessons to be taught by them to students. A no-brainer, right? Well, within the workings of the rituals of Masonry, it is not. Too often we have great ritualists that have no understanding of what the ritual is teaching to the candidate. I was recently at a lodge for a School of Instruction. Under the Grand Lodge of Tennessee, each lodge's new officers are usually instructed by a Grand Lecturer on the proper way to conduct the Tennessee Ritual. After a few months, the Grand Lecturer returns to grade the lodge on its proficiency in the ritual. At this meeting I posed the question, "What is one significance of the repeated illustration of the triangle within Masonry?" I asked the question only for the benefit of those present who were not Masonic readers. It was a room scattered with 32° Scottish Rite Masons, and the meeting was being conducted by a 33° Scottish Rite Mason. I thought at least these brethren could look at their prestigious rings and share some enlightenment. No one was able, or possibly willing, to answer the question. I made an announcement that after the meeting I would take five minutes to give a brief example of the repeated use of the triangle in Freemasonry. Only the 33° Brother, the Worshipful Master, and the Chaplain cared to show any interest. After this occurrence, I decided to write a brief article about the triangle. The product follows. It is not intended to be academic, yet I hope it serves the purpose of giving a little needed light upon a very important Masonic symbol, the triangle.

Articles in both the October and December 2005 issues of The Philalethes discuss Geometry and its application in Masonry. The principles of Geometry were held sacred by the operative masons and the ancients alike, and there is little wonder why mystical and moral symbolism and lessons have been attached to geometric figures; after all, thousands of Masons in the United States and the world over wear the initial letter of the great science as a representative of the Craft.

One geometric figure that is repeatedly illustrated within the rituals of the Craft is the triangle. The triangle is a fundamental Masonic symbol that is visible not only in the degrees of the Order, from Entered Apprentice to the higher degrees of the various obediences, but within the structure of the lodge room itself. It behooves all Master Masons with a desire to learn to examine the significance and symbology of the triangle.

Within the layout of the lodge room there are at least two prominent examples of triangles. The first is seen within the center of the lodge (this description varies by Grand Jurisdiction). In the center of the room are three lights or tapers placed in triangular form around the altar. The tapers are to be appropriately spaced in 3, 4, and 5 units. This construction creates a right triangle with the angle measurements of 37°, 53°, and 90°. The tapers represent the sun, moon, and Master of the lodge. Corresponding with these tapers are the stations of the three principal officers of the lodge: the Worshipful Master, Senior Warden, and Junior Warden, who are also in a triangular relationship with each other.

A triangle is formed by the three stationed officers when the candidate is conducted to the center of the lodge for benefit of lodge prayer in the first degree. The candidate is placed in a position bisecting the longest side. If a perpendicular were to be drawn from the candidate to the Junior Warden it would bisect the triangle formed by the officers into two right triangles with a base made by the vertices of the candidate and the Junior Warden.

As the candidate is conducted around the lodge room and presented at each station for inspection, a right triangle is formed by the principal officer of each station, the candidate, and the Senior Deacon. A triangle is also formed in all three of the Craft degrees when the candidate is conducted to the West to be instructed in how to approach the East in order to obtain light. Initially the Senior Deacon, the candidate, and the Senior Warden form a horizontal line. Upon following the instructions of the Senior Warden, the candidate takes his first, second, and/or third step(s) in Masonry. With his step(s), the candidate moves from a horizontal to form a perpendicular to the line formed by the Senior Warden and Senior Deacon. With this fluid movement the candidate has moved from a horizontal to a perpendicular to form a triangle. (Note the right angles, horizontals, and perpendiculars.)

The greatest presence of the triangle within all of Masonry is within the most recognizable symbol of the Order, the Square and Compasses. Within the Square and Compasses is present at least two dominant triangles. Within some Obediences, mostly irregular or fringe, a rule is added to the Square and Compasses bisecting them at the points where the Square and Compasses intersect. This makes readily visible an equilateral and a right triangle.

It is customary within Masonic tradition to open the compasses at a sixty degree angle when preparing the altar for all three Craft degrees. The triangle formed by the compasses and the rule has three angles all measuring 60°, an equilateral triangle. The triangle formed by the square and the rule is an isosceles right triangle, it has one angle measuring 90° and two measuring 45°.

The point within the circle alluded to within the Entered Apprentice Degree has a resonance of the triangle. This geometric figure, as well explained by Buta (2005), is an instrument made use of in order to accurately draw both equilateral and right triangles. As the Entered Apprentice Degree is an initiation into the science of Masonry, the point within a circle is an initiation into the process of constructing triangles and other geometric forms.

The most direct reference to a triangle within the three degrees is the presentation of the Forty-seventh Problem of Euclid within the Third Degree Stereoptics. The candidate is informed of Pythagoras's great travels in search of light and his presumed induction into the mysteries of secret orders, including the science of geometry and Masonry. This brief excursion is summed by telling the candidate that the symbol is to teach Masons "to be general lovers of the Arts and Sciences" (Duncan, 1976). The candidate is led to believe the inclusion of this figure in the Masonic mysteries is only as a symbol of Pythagoras's love for and acquisition of knowledge.

The afore is a collective rendition of the occurrences where the triangle is used within the Three Symbolic Degrees of Freemasonry as conferred with the York Rite Ritual. Hutchens (1995) in A Bridge to Light asserts that the triangle plays a more prominent role in the working of the Craft Degrees in the Scottish Rite system; however, this emphasis upon the Pythagorean Tetrctys is little known in the United States since virtually all Americans "take the first three degrees in York Rite lodges" (p. 33). Even so, the presence of the triangle is still undeniable. Undoubtedly there are examples of the triangle within the three degrees not related in the paragraphs above; however, for the purpose of this article, the afore illustrated examples will suffice.

The goal of this article is to provide a brief explanation of the more esoteric meaning behind the triangle. The most obvious reasoning for use of the triangle within Masonry is the use of the number three. Within Masonry there is no number that appears more often than three. A sacred number, the numeral three is repeatedly illustrated by the great lights, lesser lights, stationed officers, number of degrees, three pillars, and three sides to a triangle.

The triangle also contains the three signs mentioned within the Entered Apprentice Degree. Why should an organization affixed upon the numeral three not have as a principal symbol the geometric figure with three vertices, three sides, and three angles? In a statement representing the importance of the triangle to Masonry, Brother Albert Pike (1956) in Morals and Dogma declared that the naming of one of the Liberal Arts and Sciences geometry was a misnomer. He asserted that in the Masonic usage of geometry the more appropriate science would be trigonometry, the mathematical study of the triangle (p. 34).

Beyond this point, assumptions, theories, and postulations must be used to illustrate the triangle's significance and meaning. The following is not presented as Masonic fact, only as possible esoteric meaning. Beginning with the square and compasses, it was afore asserted that they hold both an equilateral triangle and a right triangle. The equilateral triangle is not directly mentioned or often illustrated within the Craft degrees of Masonry; however, in the higher degrees of both the York and especially the Scottish Rites the equilateral triangle is revered (Hutchens, A Bridge to Light, 1995; Hutchens, Pillars of Wisdom, 1995; Pike, 1956; Steinmetz, 1976). Steinmetz postulates that the equilateral triangle has different meaning depending upon the direction in which it points. When pointing downward, Steinmetz asserts the triangle represents Deity. When pointing in an upward direction it is a symbol of the perfect man. The brother continues to assert that the Blazing Star within the Mosaic pavement consists of two equilateral triangles, one pointing up and one pointing down representing the union of man, in a perfect state, and God (p. 87). Pike concurs that the Seal of Solomon or Star of David is a symbol of the duality and balance of man and God.

In A Bridge to Light, Hutchens (1995) states that the equilateral triangle is always a symbol of Deity (p. 23). Mackey (1927) states that the equilateral triangle was adopted by most all nations of antiquity as a symbol of Deity (p. 945). The sides of the equilateral triangle are much like the leaves of the clover. Three separate but united figures. Just as the three leaves of the clover are combined to form one plant, the three line segments of a triangle are combined to form one figure. In both cases the individual pieces represent one part of the Trinity Godhead (Father, Son, and Holy Ghost). Within the equilateral triangle each side is equal in length just as each figure in the Godhead is equal in Supremacy, separate but one, different but equal (Hutchens, 1995, A Bridge to Light). In Pillars of Wisdom, Hutchens (1995) stipulates that the purpose of opening the compasses to 60° is to symbolize Deity.

As alluded to previously, various Masonic Jurisdictions mandate that the tapers around the altar be spaced in units of 3, 4, and 5. All triangles spaced 3, 4, and 5 unit or multiples thereof are right triangles bearing the measurements afore described.

The ancients were very partial to the mystical belief in numbers. Due to this reason, "they considered the most beautiful triangle of all, the right angled triangle with sides of 3, 4, and 5 units of measure" (Hutchens, 1995, A Bridge to Light). Both Mackey (1927) and Pike (1956) assert that the sides of the sacred 3, 4, and 5 unit triangle are representative of the Egyptian deities Osiris, Isis, and Horus respectively. This assertion has a Masonic tinge in that according to myth, Osiris was killed leaving Horus a widow's son.

The relationship of Osiris, Isis, and Horus and their representation in the 3, 4, and 5 unit triangle brings the discussion to the Pythagorean Theorem. The theorem states, "the area of the square built upon the hypotenuse of a right triangle is equal to the sum of the areas of the squares upon the remaining sides" (Morris, 1997). The formula is written $a^2 + b^2 = c^2$. The theorem is most often attributed to Pythagoras; however, it is most likely that the Babylonians, a thousand years before Pythagoras, were in the possession of the knowledge (Morris). In relation to the Egyptian myth, the sum of Osiris and Isis was manifested in the being of Horus.

If this figure were representative of the 3, 4, and 5 unit right triangle of Masonic fame, the length of each side would correspond with the following: a-4 units, b-3 units, and c-5 units. Completing the formula is quite easy since the length of each side is given. The formula $a^2 + b^2 = c^2$ becomes $4^2 + 3^2 = 5^2$. After solving the squares, the problem reads $16 + 9 = 25$. The sum of 16 and 9 is 25; thusly, the sum of the area of the squares of "side a" and "side b" (25) is equal to the square of "side c", the hypotenuse (also 25).

It is repeatedly stated by many Masons and Masonic Jurisdictions that one of the principal purposes of Freemasonry is to take good men and make them better. This purpose is beautifully illustrated within the lecture and explanation of the ashlars. The goal of a Master Mason is to hewn and improve himself, breaking off the superfluous pieces and perfecting the character of man. The same illustrations could be attributed to the inclusion of triangles within the three degrees. Steinmetz (1976) asserts that the right triangle is a representation of the imperfect man and the equilateral triangle of the perfect man. The goal of a Mason is to take his imperfect state, the right triangle, and manipulate it to the formation of the perfect figure or the equilateral triangle. Two right triangles both with the angle measurements of 30°, 60°, and 90° can be placed together to form a perfect equilateral triangle.

The right triangle formed within the square and compasses may carry the same illustration. It is said by many to represent man in an imperfect state of being.

One initial thought on the inclusion of a right triangle below an equilateral triangle within the square and compasses is to symbolize the purpose of man's endeavors on Earth is to learn to subdue his passions, thereby improving himself before the world in the hope of attaining a status of perfection with God at the final day.

These are only a few of the possible meanings and interpretations of the triangle. It is hoped that this brief exploration will serve as a benefit to some inquiring Masonic mind. The reasoning and meaning behind the implementation of the triangle within the Masonic Degrees is for every Mason to interpret for himself; however, that the triangle was included and displayed within the degrees for a purpose would be very difficult to debate. There is very little that is held within the lectures, rituals, and interactions of the lodge that does not have significant meaning. Many of the symbolic meanings have been blurred and lost through the ages; however, the rich gems of purpose are still there waiting to be discovered and bring illumination to the hearts of those who are willing to journey in search of light. It not only behooves all Masons to search for these hidden meanings but it is an obligation.

References

Buta, J. (December 2005). "Esoteric geometry 101," The Philalethes, 58(6).

Duncan, M. C. (1976). Duncan's Ritual of Freemasonry. Crown, USA.

Hutchens, R. R. (1995). A Bridge to Light. The Supreme Council 33°, AASR, S.J..

Hutchens, R. R. (1995). Pillars of Wisdom. The Supreme Council 33°, AASR, S.J..

Mackey, A. G. (1927). Encyclopedia of Freemasonry and its Kindred Sciences. Philadelphia, PA: McClures Publishing Company.

Morris, S. (1997). The Pythagorean Theorem. University of Georgia, Department of Mathematics.

Pike, A. (1956). Morals and Dogma of the Ancient and Accepted Scottish Rite of Freemasonry. Richmond, VA: D. H. Jenkins, Inc.

Steinmetz, G. H. (1976). Freemasonry: Its Hidden Meaning. Macoy Publishing & Masonic Supply Co., Inc, Richmond, VA.

THE POLKS AND FREEMASONRY

By J. Rex Hartsfield

Freemasonry came to Middle Tennessee and to Maury County very early, probably with the first group of settlers. The Grand Lodge of Free and Accepted Masons of Tennessee was organized in 1813 by nine lodges who had received their charters from the Grand Lodge of North Carolina. One of these founding Lodges was Hiram Lodge #7, which is located in Franklin, and whose membership included members living in what is now Maury County. One of these members was Dr. L. B. Estes who was appointed Postmaster in Columbia, in 1807, and served until his death in 1814. When he died members of Hiram Lodge came to Columbia to conduct the Masonic Rites at his funeral. This was the first recorded Masonic meeting in Maury County.

The first organized lodge was Columbia Lodge #31 located at Columbia. This lodge was organized in 1819 and received a charter in 1820 with W. G. Dickinson serving as the charter Master. The lodge was organized and chartered with nine members and promptly initiated two additional members. This was the twelfth lodge, in Tennessee, to be chartered by the Grand Lodge of Tennessee (there were ten others chartered in surrounding states before Columbia Lodge #31 was chartered) and the Polk family became active soon after it was chartered. Masonry in Maury County grew at a fast pace and included the concordant orders of Royal Arch Masons, Royal and Select Masters and Knights Templar. From the organizing of Columbia Lodge in 1819 it grew to fourteen lodges with the last new lodge being Theta Lodge which was chartered in 1906.

Few families have, in the history of our nation, exerted the influence over events in the development of our Nation as has "The Family Polk." The influence and the contributions of the Polk Family have extended across the breadth of the country from the very beginnings of our struggle for independence until modern times. They were involved in many areas including academic, ecclesiastical, military, political and Masonic.

The first member of the Polk family came to America near the end of the seventeenth century and settled on a land grant in what is now the state of Maryland. At this time the influence and contributions of the Polk family to their adopted country began. By the middle of the eighteenth century the Polks had migrated to the Colony of North Carolina and had become involved in events which were to chart the family course for generations to come.

William Polk, of Mecklenburg County, North Carolina, had two sons, Thomas and Ezekiel. The sons of Thomas and Ezekiel, William and Samuel respectively, were to leave their marks in many areas. The accomplishments of William and Samuel and their descendants were to have a profound and lasting influence on the development of our fledgling nation and on Freemasonry in particular.

14

In the last part of the eighteenth century, the area which is now the state of Tennessee was part of North Carolina. After the Revolutionary War the new states repaid the soldiers for their war time service with land grants. Many land grants were awarded by North Carolina to soldiers and the location of the land was in "Western Carolina." Land surveying was an honorable and profitable vocation, for much of the compensation came in the form of a portion of the surveyed land. Consequently many surveyors became land speculators strictly because of the amount of land they owned as a result of their surveying activities. Both William Polk and his cousin Samuel were surveyors in Middle Tennessee. They both owned property in this section, and although William Polk did not make his permanent home here, he spent considerable time here and his sons became prominent settlers in the area. Samuel Polk, however, did settle here and became a real part of the community as did his children. The sons of William and Samuel were involved in almost every aspect of the development of what became Maury County and their influence reached out into areas of state and national arenas.

The influence and involvement of Col. William Polk and his sons extended into many areas, but it is in the Masonic realm to which this paper is directed. Col. William Polk was a member of Royal White Hart Lodge of North Carolina and was the fourth Most Worshipful Grand Master of the Grand Lodge of Ancient Free and Accepted Masons of North Carolina. He served in that capacity from December 1799 until December of 1802. It was during his term of office as Grand Master that he signed the charters for Tennessee Lodge # 41 at Knoxville and Greenville Lodge #43 at Greenville. Tennessee was, as a state, only four years old at that time and there was only one other lodge in the state. St. Tammany #29, located in Nashville, was rechartered with a name change on November 30, 1800 (also during the term of Col. William Polk) and became Harmony #1 under Tennessee. Tennessee Lodge #41 and Greenville Lodge #43 ultimately became respectfully numbers 2 and 3 when the Grand Lodge of Tennessee was organized and these three Lodges became cornerstone lodges in the formation of that Grand Lodge in 1813.

When Col. Polk signed the charters and extended Freemasonry into the newly organized state of Tennessee, I am sure that he did not realize that he was performing an act which would ultimately result in Freemasonry being projected to the shores of the Pacific Ocean and beyond. But, these lodges which formed the nucleus of the Grand Lodge of Tennessee were instrumental in the growth and expansion of Freemasonry. The members of these lodges carried Freemasonry into territories, which subsequently became part of the United States, but were unheard of and unexplored when Col. Polk signed the charters, and in some cases were colonies or territories of European countries.

In the nineteenth century the westward expansion of our country was constantly on the move. As these pioneers moved into new and uncharted areas they carried Freemasonry with them. The Grand Lodge of Tennessee chartered Lodges in Alabama, Illinois, Missouri, Arkansas, Mississippi, and California, and these lodges were instrumental in the formation of Grand Lodges. These new Grand Lodges then issued charters to lodges which were formed in new territories and states until Freemasonry reached the shores of Hawaii and the tundra of Alaska. Almost half of the states which comprise the United States can trace their Masonic Lineage directly to the Grand Lodge of Tennessee, and thus to the Grand Lodge of North Carolina and Col. William Polk.

Freemasonry was taken to the Pacific Ocean by men of the "Lewis and Clark" expedition, specifically by Meriwether Lewis and William Clark who were both masons. After this it took a somewhat slower, but steadier and more permanent movement, and The Grand Lodge of Tennessee figured very prominently in this movement as the states formed out of the "Louisiana Purchase" were settled. The lodges which formed the Grand Lodge of Missouri were originally chartered by the Grand Lodge of Tennessee, and as Missouri was the beginning of the Western Trails it also became the nearest Grand Lodge to the western territories. So it was to the Grand Lodge of Missouri that charter applications were made when new lodges were formed in the territories.

This paper is principally devoted to the Masonic involvements of the immediate families of William Polk and Samuel Polk in Maury County and is still very much "a work in progress" as there is still much research to be done. Columbia Lodge #31 was the first lodge in the area, and it was in Columbia Lodge that the Polks were to become members. Columbia Lodge was chartered in 1820 and many of the earlier records are no longer available, as some were destroyed by the invading Armies and some were lost when the Masonic Hall was damaged in the fire of 1946. Lafayette Chapter #4 of Royal Arch Masons was chartered in 1825, Concordia Council #2 of R & S.M. was chartered in 1849 and DeMolay Commandery #3 was chartered in 1859. The records of Lafayette Chapter are intact and reveal a part of the growth and history of Maury County, but because they surrendered their charters the records of Concordia Council and Demolay Commandery are archived at the Tennessee Grand Lodge office in Nashville.

Col. William Polk had nine sons and at least four of these sons were active in Masonry in Middle Tennessee. They became members of existing Masonic organizations and were instrumental in organizing and chartering new ones.

Their influence and involvement in Masonic affairs extended far beyond the local area of Middle Tennessee. They helped to form state level Masonic organizations, and these organizations then issued charters to form local Masonic bodies in the states and territories being established by the western migration. His sons were:

• Dr. William Polk was an early member of Columbia Lodge #31 and may have been a charter member of this lodge.

• Lucius Junius Polk—First Commander and organizer of Demolay Commandery #3 of Knights Templar in Columbia, Tennessee. This Commandery was organized in 1858 largely due to his efforts. He represented DeMolay Commandery #3 at a meeting in Nashville which resulted in the formation of the Grand Commandery of Tennessee. He subsequently served as the second Grand Commander of the Grand Commandery of Tennessee. His major contribution in assisting to organize the Grand Commandery of Tennessee was to serve as Chairman of the committee to write the Constitution and By-Laws. His name first appears on lodge records as being a member of Columbia Lodge in 1825. He also became a member of Lafayette Chapter #4 of Royal Arch Masons in 1825 and Concordia Council of Royal and Select Masters, both located here in Columbia. After its formation he became a member of Euphemia Lodge #195, in Columbia, and was a member of that lodge at his death in 1870. Lucius also served several terms on the Board of Trustees of various Educational Institutions, including Jackson College.

• Leonidas Polk—I have found no record, as of yet, that Leonidas was a Mason, but his father, his brothers and many of his close friends and associates, including his friend and mentor Bishop James Otey, were members. (this is one area I am researching).

• Rufus K. Polk—I believe he, too, was a member of Columbia Lodge #31 and Lafayette Chapter, but his death in 1843 and his membership in the lodge would have been during the period of time for which I have not located the records.

• George W. Polk—Who originally became a member of Columbia Lodge, but became a Charter member of Euphemia Lodge #195 when that lodge was formed in 1850. He remained a member of Euphemia Lodge until that lodge surrendered its Charter in 1887, at which time he affiliated again with Columbia Lodge and remained a member of that lodge, Lafayette Chapter #4 of Royal Arch Masons and Concordia Council #2 until his death. Part of the lore of Maury County is that Rattle and Snap was spared the torch because the Union officer saw a Masonic ring on his finger in his portrait which was hanging in the entry hall, and being himself a Mason he spared the house. George W. Polk also served on the Board of Trustees of Jackson College.

• Andrew J. Polk—Originally became a member of Columbia Lodge #31, but became a member of and served as Charter Junior Warden of Euphemia Lodge #195 when it was formed in 1850. He was also a member of Lafayette Chapter #4, Concordia Council #2 and Demolay Commandery #3. He remained a member of those organizations until he left the country to live in Europe and his membership is unknown after that. He also served on the Board of Trustees of Jackson College.

•   The sons of William Polk were instrumental in the formation and chartering of Euphemia Lodge #195 and most of the other members of the lodge were from their close circle of friends. Francis G. Roche was the charter Master of the lodge and was the manager of the old State Bank; E.H. Cressey was the Senior Warden of the new lodge and he was Rector of St Johns Church and Principal of Ashwood School for Girls. Many names from the list of prominent Maury County citizens were found on the membership list of Euphemia Lodge including the Pillows, Coopers, Devereuxs and Porter to name a few. These were also the same men who served on various Boards and directed the affairs of the city and county. Bishop Otey was not only a mentor for Leonidas Polk, but college classmate of Lucius Polk and a member of Hiram Lodge in Franklin. He also served as Grand Chaplain of both the Grand Lodge and Grand Chapter of Royal Arch Masons of Tennessee. They were also instrumental in, and supported the Masonic organizations of Maury County when they purchased Jackson College. This school was purchased from the Presbyterian Church in 1848 for the sum of $5,500.00. The purchase price was raised by the Masonic organizations and the various organizations received shares according to the amount of their investment. Jackson College was operated by a President who was subject to a Board of Trustees who were elected to the positions by the individual organization. The school was in operation until it was burned by Union soldiers in 1863. The County Masonic organizations then disposed of the rubble and stone, but still had a Board to oversee their interest in the property until after 1900.

Samuel Polk had at least three sons and one son-in-law who were active in Masonry:

•James Knox Polk – his oldest son was an active member and officer of Columbia Lodge #31 and of Lafayette Chapter #4 of Royal Arch Masons of Columbia, Tennessee. James Knox Polk received his Masonic degrees in Columbia Lodge #31 in 1820 and was one of the first members to receive the Royal Arch degrees in the newly formed Lafayette Chapter #4 in Columbia in 1825.

18

He carried the teachings and tenets of Masonry with him throughout a life in public service at the local, state and national levels. His decision to become a Mason was undoubtedly influenced by his esteem for Felix Grundy and Andrew Jackson, both of whom were ardent Masons and his political and professional mentors. His call to public service precluded a real active involvement in anything else, but he attended Columbia Lodge and Lafayette Chapter whenever his duties allowed him to take the time. There are entries in the minutes of Lafayette Chapter where he served as both an installed officer and as a Pro tem officer. I read in one source that he was an elected officer of Columbia Lodge, but I haven't verified that. The last record I have found of his attendance at a Masonic meeting in Columbia was when he attended a meeting of Lafayette Chapter in 1842. This would have been between his term as Governor and his Presidential term. James K. Polk apparently enjoyed being a Mason and enjoyed participating in Masonic activities. He did take time from his presidential duties to participate in two cornerstone ceremonies while he was President—the laying of the cornerstone of the Washington Monument and of the Smithsonian Institute.

•William Hawkins Polk was the ninth child and fifth son of Samuel Polk and was a member of Columbia Lodge #31, Lafayette Chapter #4 Royal Arch Masons and Demolay Commandery #3 of Knights Templar.

•Franklin E. Polk—The fourth child and second son of Samuel Polk was a member of Columbia Lodge #31.

•James Walker, who was married to Jane Maria Polk (Samuel Polk's oldest daughter), was a member and active in Columbia Lodge #31 and also in Lafayette Chapter #4.

Several members of subsequent Polk generations, including Lucius Polk, Jr. and Horace Polk, have been members and served various Masonic organizations in Maury County in elective and appointive offices. James Knox Polk, son of William Hawkins Polk was a member of Phoenix Lodge in Nashville and also of the York Rite Bodies in Nashville. I am sure there were other members of the Polk family who were Masons, but I am still researching and will probably have to go out of the state of Tennessee to find some of the information.

References

Polk, William R. Polk's Folly, An American Family History. New York: Anchor Books, 2000.

Snodgrass, Charles A. and Bobby J. Demott. The History of Freemasonry in Tennessee. Knoxville: Tennessee Valley Publishing, 1994.

Excerpts of The History of the Grand Lodge of North Carolina (available at Tennessee State Library and Archives).

Maury County Archives, Columbia, Tennessee.

Minutes of Columbia Lodge #31 F& A.M. Columbia, Tennessee.

Minutes of Euphemia Lodge #195 F & A. M. Columbia, Tennessee.

Minutes of LaFayette Chapter #4 R.A.M. Columbia, Tennessee.

Proceedings of the Grand Lodge of Free and Accepted Masons of Tennessee.

PARALLELS OF FREEMASONRY AND PLATO'S ALLEGORY OF THE CAVE

By Dr. David E. Stafford

Throughout history there have been many men who have attained a stature of high regard in the halls of Freemasonry. These men were usually individuals who added great triumphs to the world about them whether it be socially, academically, philosophically, or masonically. Each of these men may not have been raised in the Order but are believed to have been prepared and made a Mason in his heart. These are men who embraced the enlightenment thought either with or without the guidance of the Craft. One such man is the great philosophical teacher Plato. In the writings of Brother Albert Pike, Plato's time honored teachings are allured to repeatedly. Some Masonic authors even attribute a veiled lineage to the philosophical academies of Plato's time. Of all his writings, there is at least one lesson from this great educator's repertoire that has parallels with the system of Freemasonry. Plato's Allegory of the Cave should have great Masonic resonance for all who have been inducted into the roll of the Craft.

Before undertaking the task of exploring the parallels between Freemasonry and Plato's Allegory of the Cave, it is prudent to examine what, if any, connection Plato has with the Craft and its development. First and foremost, it is important to assert, at the onset of this exploration, that there will be no claim that Plato was inducted into the mysteries of Freemasonry or that it traces its lineage from his, or any other, ancient mystery school. This examination will only look at what the shapers and formers of modern Freemasonry thought about and gleaned from Plato's writings and example. Any obvious connections that can be drawn between Plato's Allegory of the Cave and the modern institution of Free and Accepted Masonry will also be reviewed.

Plato's Life and Academy

Although there is some debate as to the date of Plato's birth, it is generally accepted that he was born around the year 428 BC (Guthrie, 1979). His given name was Aristocles. The name Plato was seemingly a nickname meaning broad, perhaps in reference to his physical appearance. Plato's early life is blurred by antiquity and unreliable accounts. His immediate family, while politically connected and affluent, was not overly impressive, and Plato most likely lived an early life of little difficulty (Guthrie).

Plato was a student of the acclaimed teacher Socrates. This relationship was very impressing upon the life and personal views of Plato. Perhaps the most influential experience in Plato's life was the death of his revered teacher. According to Nails (2002), Plato was twenty-eight when Socrates was condemned to death by drinking the notorious hemlock. Following Socrates' death, Plato left Athens and traveled to Megara, Cyrene, Italy, Sicily, and Egypt (McEvoy, 1984). It is during this time of travel that, according to Wilmshurst (1922), Plato sought initiation into the Egyptian Mysteries but was rejected by the high priest. "You Greeks are but children in the Secret Doctrine" Sais, the priest, was reported to have replied to Plato's requests to being inducted into the mysteries. The ancients, according to tradition, did instruct Plato in the sacred and spiritual doctrines, and he was advanced in knowledge and understanding of the ancient mysteries.

Following his travels and intellectual search for light, Plato returned to Athens around the age of forty, and he established a school, the Academy, in the Grove of Academus (Cairn, 1961). Plato's school was geographically located within a grove or a public park filled with gymnasiums, altars, statues, and temples. Plato's Academy most probably was a loose connection of men who came to learn criticism of method by listening to his dialogues and instruction. The leader or head of the Academy was apparently elected for life by the majority vote of its members. Plato remained the Head of the Academy until his death in 348/347 BC. It was in the Academy that Plato instructed some of the greatest intellectual minds of Western Civilization, including Aristotle.

Ancient and Masonic Writers and Plato

The Illustrious Brother Albert Pike, who incidentally was called by some the "Plato of Freemasonry," held the teachings of Plato in high esteem (Hall, 2006). In Morals and Dogma, Pike (1956) reveals his position that Plato is among the greatest revelers of truth and light. Pike stated that Plato expounded and expressed the noble doctrine of nature "in the most beautiful and luminous manner" (p. 617).

Wilmshurst (1922) refers to Plato in his revered work The Meaning of Masonry. Wilmshurst stated that in order to fully understand the Fellow Craft Degree, a student of Freemasonry must study two ancient sources. The first of these is Plato's Dialogues. "The other is the records of the classical Christian contemplatives . . . ." (p. 123). Of interest is Wilmshurst's reminder to the reader that Plato refers to the four cardinal virtues in Phædo and the Book of Wisdom, ch. viii, 5-7. If the studying Mason researches this point, he will not find the traditional Masonic virtues of fortitude, prudence, temperance, and justice. Instead he would find justice, temperance, wisdom, and courage.

22

Mackey (1882) in The Symbolism of Freemasonry stated, "And Plato says that the design of initiation was to restore the soul to that state of perfection from which it had originally fallen". This being taken from the Phædo, it is evident the general esoteric goal of both the ancient mysteries and modern Freemasonry are similar in concept.

The Dionysian Artificers refers to Plato numerous times. The work points out the importance of understanding that fables and allegories often contain numerous meanings (De Costa, 1936). It further asserted that Plato's teaching of "the descent of the soul into the darkness of the body, the perils of the passions, [and] the torments of vices" are shared by Virgil and illustrated in writings (p. 22). Of these, the descent of the soul into the darkness is relevant to the topic at hand. Fakhry (2004) connects the Allegory of the Cave and Ibn Sina's Allegory of the Bird. Fakhry asserted that both illustrate the destiny of the soul to only be released from bondage through an attainment of knowledge. It is recommended that all seek out and study the Allegory of the Bird. It has meaning and purpose to all men, but without a doubt it has great importance and is worthy of examination by those who are called seekers of light.

An Initial Examination

In the centuries between Plato's first oration of the afore described allegory and today, there have been countless numbers of interpretations of its meaning. Nearly every civilized culture and society has examined and synthesized the allegory to extract meaning and support to their lives. It is this allegory's ability to be interpreted in varied ways that makes it such a fundamental and enduring legacy of the thoughts and teachings of Plato. Why then should it not be appropriate to ascertain a Masonic interpretation of Plato's Allegory of the Cave?

The allegory's first element of Masonic resonance is its ability to be interpreted in varied ways. Just as it is asserted that the allegory's ability to be varied in interpretation has added to its popularity and survival, the same may be said of Freemasonry. No institution which is austere, unbending, and disobliging can have a true global existence, spanning geographic, religious, political, and cultural boundaries. It is the ability of Freemasonry to meet the needs of men from all creeds and walks of life that has led to its survival over the centuries. Without this ability to be relevant to Christians, Muslims, Jews, Buddhists, and Deists alike both the allegory of the Cave and Freemasonry would either be isolated or lost in the ages of time.

In From Socrates to Sartre: The Philosophic Quest, Dr. T. Z. Lavine (1984) of George Washington University describes the allegory in such a way that one could use the same sentences to describe the Craft itself. "It is

23

an allegory of our time as needing to be born again, to emerge from the darkness of corruption into the light of truth and morality. It is an educational allegory of our time as needing to ascend through stages of education from the darkness of intellectual and moral confusion in its everyday beliefs, to the light of true knowledge and values" (p. 28). Freemasonry hopes to lead its initiates to higher understandings of truth and life, to put away the dim light of superstition and passion, to embrace the illumination of reason, intellectual knowledge, an immutable values. Dr. Lavine's brief interpretations of the allegory provide a Masonic aura and a spring board for its analysis.

Both Freemasonry and Plato's allegory begin with men in a darkened condition. The men in the cave are groping in darkness and bound to the blighted beliefs of superstition and self-prescribed truths. It is noteworthy to point out that the allegory takes place within a cave. Caverns have long been considered, masonically, to be "a symbol of the darkness of ignorance and crime impenetrable to the light of truth" (Mackey, 1927, p. 169). In the Ninth degree of the Scottish Rite, "the cave is a symbol of the imprisonment of the human soul and intellect by ignorance, superstition, deceit, and fraud" (Hutchens, 2000). The neophyte, who has petitioned Freemasonry, is held in the bondage of ignorance just as the mass of mankind is held in ignorance to the great and true teachings of the Craft. "There disinterestedness vanishes, every one howls, searches, gropes, and gnaws for himself. Ideas are ignored, and of progress there is no thought" (Pike, 1956, p. 3). Just as the profane is satisfied by the broken image of himself, so are the individuals in the cave content with living in darkness without any hope of intellectual growth or true fulfillment. It is also noteworthy to point out that the three ruffians, in the Ninth degree, are found hiding in a cave. Where else do ignorance, tyranny, and fanaticism belong?

In his allegory, Plato presents us with a very interesting assertion. He presents an occurrence where all the prisoners are released to turn and see the images within the cave. As they view the darkness around them, their eyes are not able to adjust to the protruding and offensive brightness of the fire's light. They quickly become disillusioned and repulsed by the image and desire to return to their once darkened condition. Does this image not hold great Masonic meaning? The totality of the prisoners represents the mass of mankind. Brother Pike (1956) in Morals and Dogma states "people, as a mass, (are) rude and unorganized" (p. 6). Mankind, as an innate passion, loves squalor and ignorance. It is only through the instruction of an agent, such as Freemasonry, that the individual, not the mass, can be raised above his inborn breeding and grow intellectually, to grasp its rich meaning and hidden gems of purpose. It is only the few, the minority of intellectually prone individuals, who can be lifted up from the mire of mankind's filth to be bettered by the teachings of the Craft.

The mass would be unable to perceive the teachings of the allegories of Masonry and would quickly be blinded and wish to return to their previous status in life. As the Hebrew proverb states, "As a dog returneth to his vomit, so a fool returneth to his folly."

Freemasonry has always known that the masses are not compatible with its teachings; therefore, it has only admitted the best and most lofty individuals of society to attain the progressive instruction it has to offer. The degrees of the Craft are only represented within Plato's allegory when considering the individual, just as only one man should be introduced to the mysteries of Masonry at a time. Within the lodge, the uninitiated is hoodwinked and blinded to the occurrences about him. He is kept in darkness for two reasons. The first reason is a reminder of the vow of secrecy soon to be taken. Secondly, it is intended that the candidate for the Entered Apprentice Degree, and all others, perceive the forms of the lodge in his heart before he views the beauties thereof with his eyes. The individual in Plato's allegory is kept in darkness to reality. During this time, he uses shadows and distorted noises to conceive the reality that is around him, and the proselyte is not brought to light until after his cable tow has been removed. In the allegory, the prisoner is not brought to light until his shackles are opened. The agent who brings him to initial light walks him around the cave and points to objects and demands the individual to name them (Plato). The parallel exists that neither the individual released from bondage nor the newly made brother within the lodge are brought to complete light. The teachings of both are only partial. The two initiates are allowed to adjust to the new light that has been shown them and expected to progress through further stages to attain more light and greater understanding.

The next development in the journey of a man seeking Masonic enlightenment occurs through the teachings and philosophy of the Fellow Craft's Degree. This second degree of Masonry is filled with great and enduring ideas and teachings for the neophyte seeking further light in the Craft. The legend of the winding staircase holds lessons of the utmost importance, and within its beautifully illustrated lessons lie one word that most suitably expresses its meaning. That single word is ascension. The passage taken to the Holy of Holies is sacred and dominated by the ascension of a winding staircase. This winding staircase is symbolic of the journey of one seeking a liberal education (Mackey, 1927). Mackey explains, "the path of the Fellow Craft requires him to ascend, step by step, until he has reached the summit, where the treasures of knowledge await him" (p. 1007). Education is the great equalizer and is the one thing that a man can do to elevate himself above others. H. L. Haywood (1922) stresses the second degree's importance in elevating men intellectually. All men who seek elevation are destined to ascend the enlightened path of knowledge. Education and academics are the paths by which Masonry teaches one must take to truly find enlightenment. The experience of the freedman, within Plato's allegory, being dragged from the darkness of the cave can be compared to the winding staircase of the second degree. It is through this ascending passage that he finds the most brilliant light. The contradiction between the allegory and the second degree is the fact that the individual in the allegory is "reluctantly dragged up a steep and rugged ascent" (Plato). Freemasonry never forces itself upon initiates. It is through one's own freewill and accord that an individual is exposed to the teachings of the Craft.

"When he approaches the light his eyes will be dazzled, and he will not be able to see anything at all of what are now called realities" (Plato). This passage is true for both the allegory and the newly passed Fellow Craft. In each degree of Freemasonry, the brilliant light to which the candidate is exposed is so bright he at first is blinded by it. It might be prescribed that for this reason a period of at least twenty-eight days, in most jurisdictions, and a lecture are required before advancement might be made. This allotted time allows maturation of and ample reflection upon the seeds sewn within the lessons of the degree (Driber, 2004).

It is through the maturation of a candidate spiritually and intellectually, his listening to the instruction of well informed brethren, and the reflection upon the lessons taught him that a man is prepared to experience the life changing episode of the Third Degree of Masonry. Only after a candidate has first been brought to light and shown the initial beauties of the lodge and passed through the ascension of growth intellectually that a man can be raised to the newness of life as a Master Mason. The same journey, symbolically and allegorically, had to occur to the released prisoner. He had to first be brought to the understanding that he was in a state of bondage, after which he was caused to pass through the ascension of knowledge to seek the bright light at the pinnacle of the summit. It is at this summit that the freedman is truly brought to full illumination and entitled to freely see the realities of the world about him.

"First he will see the shadows best, next the reflections of men and other objects in the water, and then the objects themselves; then he will gaze upon the light of the moon and the stars and the spangled heaven; and he will see the sky and the stars by night better than the sun or the light of the sun by day? Last of all he will be able to see the sun, and not mere reflections of him in the water, but he will see him in his own proper place, and not in another; and he will contemplate him as he is" (Plato). Through the lessons of the Third Degree a man is shown his place in the world as an immortal being destined to be resurrected by the ultimate Creator. The teachings of the Third Degree are explained to the newly raised brother; however, the truer and deeper realities and meanings of the degree are much later discovered, if ever. The freed prisoner in Plato's allegory is able to view all the glories of the real world once he has completed his ascent from the cave; so too, the Master Mason is entitled and does receive a full explanation of the mysteries of Craft Masonry. Neither individual is at once able to comprehend the beauties he is caused to behold. It is through the reflection and consistent study upon what is seen and experienced that the true lessons are learned by both.

Other Writers' Parallels

Fanthrope and Fanthorpe (2006) stated that the Allegory of the Cave illustrates "the significance of free and independent thought as a pathway to truth" (p.110). They continued to state that the prisoner who first escaped "from the cave of deceptive shadows and discovered reality is someone who has learned Masonic truth" (p. 110). According to the authors, Plato taught the things we see, touch, smell, and hear are not reality. They assert that Plato believed that all that we perceive with our senses must be elevated through the mind before true understanding can occur. It was, according to Plato, the role of the philosopher to help others release the light within his students to allow them to understand the world around them through a stimulated mind. Fanthrope and Fanthorpe allude to the conclusion that this goal is shared with Freemasonry.

Conclusions

It is not suggested that the intent of The Allegory of the Cave was meant to be an illustration of Freemasonry. The absurdity of such an assertion would be a gross injustice to the honor of the fraternity. It is also acknowledged that many works of literature and philosophy could be stretched to illustrate some Masonic teaching. It is hoped, those who read this will find it Masonically enlightening rather than a mere stretch of Masonic thought. The thought Plato tried to impart through his allegory clearly parallels the high teachings of the Craft. It is only natural for an institution defined as "a peculiar system of morality veiled in allegory and illustrated by symbols" to be interested in the parallels of those great minds who so effectively used allegories as tools of instruction. We are taught in the Second Degree of Freemasonry to cultivate the Arts and to grow in usefulness. This can only be achieved through consistent and intense reflection upon the Craft, and by paralleling and searching the philosophies and ideals that so closely resemble the morals of the Craft. May the Order of Freemasonry be as enduring as the teachings of the great philosopher Plato.

References

Cairns, H. (1961). Introduction to Plato: The Collected Dialogues, Princeton University Press.

DeCosta, H. J. (1936). The Dionysian Artificers, Philosophical Research Society, Retrieved from http://www.sacred-texts.com/cla/dart/index. htm.

Driber, T. J. (2004). Why we wait a minimum of 28 days. Tennessee Lodge of Research F & AM Annual Proceeding, 2004.

Fanthorpe, L. & Fanthorpe, P. (2006). Mysteries and Secrets of the Masons: The Story Behind the Masonic Order. Dundurn Press Ltd.

Fakhry, M. (2004). A History of Islamic Philosophy. Columbia University Press.

Guthrie, W. K. C. (1979) A History of Greek Philosophy, vol. 4, Cambridge University Press.

Hall, M. P. (2006). The Phoenix: An Illustrated Review of Occultism and Philosophy. Kessinger Publishing.

Haywood, H. L. (1922). The Great Teachings of Masonry. Kingsport, TN: Southern Publishers.

Lavine, T. Z. (1984). From Socrates to Sartre: The Philosophic Quest. New York, NY: Bantam Books.

Mackey, A. G. (1927). Encyclopedia of Freemasonry and its Kindred Sciences. Philedelphia, PA: McClures Publishing Company.

McEvoy, J. (1984). "Plato and The Wisdom of Egypt". Irish Philosophical Journal, (1)2.

Nails, D. (2002). The People of Plato: A Prosopograghy and Other Socratics. Indianapolic, IN: Hackett Publishing Company.

Pike, A. (1956). Morals and Dogma of the Ancient and Accepted Scottish Rite of Freemasonry. Richmond, VA: D. H. Jenkins, Inc..

Plato. The Republic, Book VII. Retrieved from: http://www.sacred-texts. com/cla/plato/rep/rep0700.htm.

Wilmshurst, W. L. (1922). The Meaning of Masonry. P. Lund, Humphries and Company, London.

CHEVALIER ANDREW MICHAEL RAMSAY
AND THE KNIGHTS TEMPLAR

By George C. Ladd III

Shortly after I was raised to the sublime degree of Master Mason, I read the book, Born in Blood, by our late Brother John G. Robinson. In his book Brother Robinson told the fascinating and engaging story of the Knights Templar, and what he perceived was a close relationship between that Order of crusader knights and the forms and ceremonies of Freemasonry. I found Brother Robinson's case persuasive, and was satisfied, after reading Born in Blood, that Freemasonry more or less came from the Knights Templar.

Then I joined the Philalethes Society, an international Masonic research society. One of the benefits of membership in that organization is its listserv, that is, an e-mail discussion group whereby one sends e-mail to the listserv and it is disseminated to everyone who subscribes to the group, not unlike Yahoo Groups, and thereby creates an international discussion of Masonic matters and topics. When I encountered their first discussion of the Knights Templar since my joining the group, I discovered that very few of the scholars on that list gave credence to Robinson's theories, nor did any of the Philalethes Brethren who were active on that list believe that Masonry came from the Knights Templar.

I recall one Brother on the list asserted that we know when the notion of a connection between Masonry and the Knights Templar started, by whom, and for what purpose. The notion was started, claimed this Brother, by Chevalier Andrew Michael Ramsay, in Paris in 1737 in a lecture which was published in 1741 under the title Discourse Pronounced at the Reception of a Freemason. (1) This Brother claimed it was done for the purpose of encouraging Catholics to become Masons.

Leaving aside the merits of the theories of John G. Robinson, Brothers Knight and Lomas (who wrote The Hiram Key), Baigent and Leigh (who wrote Holy Blood, Holy Grail), and Dan Brown (who wrote The Da Vinci Code), here is the story of Chevalier Andrew Michael Ramsay and his famous lecture that, according to some, is the spark that ignited the fire that led to the founding of the Masonic Knights Templar and, some argue, the French Hauts Grades, or "High Degrees" which ultimately evolved into the Ancient and Accepted Scottish Rite.

Ramsay was born in Ayr, Scotland, between 1680 and 1688. He entered the University of Edinburgh at the age of 14. In 1706, he left for Europe. In 1710, he became impressed with the Quietist philosophy and, though previously a Calvinist, joined the Roman Catholic Church. (2)

Quietism states that man's highest perfection consists of a self-annihilation, and subsequent absorption, of the soul into the Divine, even during the present life. In this way, the mind is withdrawn from worldly interests to passively and constantly contemplate God. (3)

In Paris, in 1723, Ramsay became the tutor to the young Duc de Chateau-Thierry, and the Regent, Philippe d'Orleans, conferred upon Ramsay the Order of St. Lazarus, which bestowed on Ramsay the title of "Chevalier," or Knight.

In 1724, in Rome, he became the tutor of Bonnie Prince Charles and his brother, and was their tutor for 15 months. In 1725, interestingly, he was offered the position of tutor to the son of the King of England, but refused, saying that "he was a Roman Catholic and not suited to a place in a Protestant king's household." (4)

In 1727 he gained literary fame when he published The Travels of Cyrus. He moved to England in 1728, and the London Evening Post for March 17, 1729 reports that "On Monday night last at the Horn Lodge in the Palace Yard, Westminster (whereof his Grace the Duke of Richmond is Master) there was a numerous appearance of persons of distinction at which time... the Chevalier Ramsay" (along with a number of other distinguished persons listed) "...were admitted members of the Ancient Society of Free and Accepted Masons." In that same year, he was elected a Fellow of the Royal Society. In 1730 he received his Doctor of Civil Law Degree from Oxford University, becoming the first Roman Catholic to receive a degree at Oxford since the English Reformation of 1535.

Ramsay returned to France where, on March 20, 1737, as Grand Chancellor or Grand Orator of some Masonic body in Paris, Ramsay delivered, or at least prepared, a discourse or lecture or charge to be given as part of a Masonic initiation. According to Coil's Encyclopedia, "it is the earliest known exposition of the alleged connection between Freemasonry and the Knights Templar or other Crusaders, the theme which formed the basis for the later Hauts Grades (or "High Degrees"). The full text of the lecture is printed in Gould's History of Freemasonry. What follows is Coil's paraphrase of the lecture from which, according to Coil, "the general sense and effect of the discourse can be better obtained than from the too ornate language of the author."

"The noble ardour which you, gentlemen, evince to enter into the most noble and very illustrious order of Freemasons, is a certain proof that you already possess all the qualities necessary to become members, that is, humanity, pure morals, inviolable secrecy and a taste for the fine arts."

He continued: *"The world is nothing but a huge republic, of which every nation is a family and every individual a child. Our Society was established to revive and spread these essential maxims. We desire to reunite all men, not only by love of the fine arts, but by the principles of virtue, science, and religion, whereby the interests of the Fraternity shall become those of the whole human race and whence all nations will draw knowledge, and their subjects will cherish one another, without renouncing their own country. The Grand Masters of Germany, Italy, England, and elsewhere have arranged for the publication of a Universal Dictionary of the arts and sciences, excepting theology and politics, and the work is already begun in London. Our ancestors, the Crusaders, desired thus to unite in one Fraternity the individuals of all nations, and we owe it to them to carry out the project. Our ancestors, the Crusaders, desired to change a sad, savage, and misanthropic philosophy into one of innocent pleasures, agreeable music, pure joy, and moderate gaiety. Our secrets are the words of war which the Crusaders used to distinguish their companions and to detect Saracen foes. Our founders were not simple workers in stone, nor yet curious geniuses; they were not only skilled architects, engaged in the construction of material temples, but also religious and warrior princes who designed to enliven, edify and protect the living Temples of the Most High. The Crusaders vowed to restore the Temple of the Christians in the Holy Land. They agreed upon several ancient signs and symbolic words, and the promise to keep them secret was a bond to unite Christians of all nationalities in one fraternity. Our Order then made union with the Knights of St. John of Jerusalem, hence, the name, Lodges of St. John. This union was made after the example of the Israelites in the erection of the Second Temple, who, while they handled the trowel and mortar with one hand, in the other, they held the sword and buckler. Our Order, therefore, was founded in remote antiquity and renewed in the Holy Land. Returning from Palestine, the kings, princes, and lords, established lodges, first, in Germany, Italy, Spain, France, and, thence, in Scotland, because of the close alliance between the French and the Scotch. James, Lord Steward of Scotland, was Grand Master at Kilwinning in 1286. Prince Edward (Edward I), son of Henry III of England, brought his defeated troops back from the eighth and last Crusade and established them in a colony in England, and declared himself protector, whereupon, this Fraternity took the name, Freemasons. Since that time, England has been the seat of the Order, but the religious discord which tore Europe in the 16th century caused our Order to degenerate from the nobility of its origin. The rites are changed, disguised, and suppressed. From the British Isles, the Royal Art is now repassing to France, which being one of the most spiritual in Europe will become center of the Order. She will clothe our work, our statutes, and our customs with grace, delicacy, and good taste, essential qualities of the Order of which the basis is wisdom, strength, and beauty."* *"Yes, Sirs, the famous festivals of Ceres at Eleusis, of Isis in Egypt, of Minerva at Athens, of Urania amongst the Phoenicians, of Diana in Scythia, were connected with ours. In those places mysteries were celebrated which arrested many vestiges of the ancient religion of Noah and the Patriarchs. They concluded with banquets and libations where neither the impertinence nor excess were known into which the heathen gradually fell. The source of these infamies was the admission to the nocturnal assemblies of persons of both sexes in contravention of the primitive usages. It is in order to prevent similar abuse that women are excluded from our Order. We are not so unjust as to regard the fair sex as incapable of keeping a secret. But their presence might insensibly corrupt the purity of our maxims and manners."* (5)

It is not certain whether Ramsay ever delivered this lecture. On March 20, 1737, the day before the lecture was to be delivered, Ramsay wrote a note to the Prime Minister to the King of France, Cardinal Fleury, asking the Cardinal to give his support to the Society of Freemasons. The note stated "As I am to read my discourse tomorrow in a general assembly of the Order and to hand it on Monday to the examiners of the Chancellerle [censors of the press], I pray your Excellency to return it to me tomorrow before mid-day by express messenger." On March 22, the day after the Masonic meeting, Ramsay wrote "I learn that the assemblies of the Freemasons displease your Excellency. I have never frequented them except with a view of spreading maxims which would by degrees render incredulity ridiculous, vice odious, and ignorance shameful. I am persuaded that if men of your Excellency's choice were introduced to head these assemblies, they would become very useful to religion, the state and literature, etc." According to Coil, Fleury wrote in pencil in the margin of that letter "The King does not wish it."

In response to this, Ramsay may not have actually delivered his Discourse, and nothing more was heard of Ramsay during the remaining 6 years of his life. After his death, his wife and friends edited and published his finest work, The Philosophical Principles of Natural and Revealed Religion, unfolded in Geometrical Order, in his words, "a history of the human mind in all ages, nations and religions concerning the most divine and important truths."

Coil opines that "No other Freemason ever gained so much prominence in so short a time with so little effort and maintained his position so long!" Coil was not certain whether Ramsay inspired and influenced the creation of the Hauts Grades, with their Chivalric and Crusader themes, or whether the early Hauts Grades influenced Ramsay. Ultimately, according to Coil, over 1100 High Degrees were created in 100 rites. (6)

Our Canadian Brother Stephen Dafoe, who has written five books dealing with the Knights Templar, asserts that "although Ramsay did not tie a Masonic apron around the Templars' waist, he did connect the Freemasons with the Order of the Hospitallers; and it was for this reason, Ramsay claimed, that Masonic lodges were dedicated to Saint John.

It would be the German Freemasons who add the Templar angle via the Rite of Strict Observance, which started in the late 1740s. The German Masons made the claim that when the Templars had occupied the Temple of Solomon, they acquired magical powers and secret wisdom, which Jacques de Molay passed on to his successor prior to his execution."

Dafoe continues: "There was also the claim that the Templar torch was passed to Pierre d'Aumont, who had fled to Scotland, where the exiled Templars established Freemasonry. From Scotland it returned to France and thence on to Germany. In Scandanavian countries, the Masons drew their lineage through the Order of Christ in Portugal,... that de Molay's nephew had carried his ashes to Stockholm, buried them there, and later on established the Swedish Templar order. There was also the claim that the Templars had assisted Robert the Bruce in the Battle of Bannockburn, who later established the Order of Heredom on their behalf as a repayment."

Dafoe asserts "none of these accounts had a kernel of truth in them, but as the Masonic author Burton E. Bennett wrote in 1926:

These fabrications were made for the purpose of establishing an Order not only that nobles of all countries could join, but that all who joined would believe they became ennobled. Designing men took advantage of it to obtain both money and power through the 'lost secrets,' occultism and magic. It was an age that believed not only with personal contact with God, but also with the devil; and the supposed secrets of the Ancient Masons furnished the seed for all this tremendous growth."

Dafoe has a new book, to be published this year, entitled The Compasses and the Cross: A History of the Masonic Knights Templar. (7)

According to Coil, the first documented reference to a Masonic Templar degree or ceremony is in the records of Andrew's Royal Arch Chapter at Boston, Massachusets, on August 28, 1769, when "Bro. William Davis... was made by receiving the four steps, that of Excellent, Super-excellent, Royal Arch, and Knight Templar." The next oldest reference is a warrant issued by the Master of Kilwinning Lodge, Scotland, to the High Knights Templar of Ireland Lodge on Oct. 8, 1779. (8)

What if, contrary to Born in Blood, there is no causal connection between Masonry and the Knights Templar? What if the connection between Masonry and the Templars is only a lecture (or the notes of a lecture), to have been given one night in Paris in 1737? Even if there is no causal connection between the Templars and the Masons, the Poor Fellow Soldiers of Christ and the Temple of Solomon are still worth my attention, my respect, and my affection.

I will still "claim kin" to these noble warrior monks. Those facts of history communicated by Robinson are fascinating. At the very least, I am made aware of this noble Order and its history during and after the Crusades; a history which is fascinating and inspiring in its own right, and worth my time, my study, and my profound respect. At the center of their story is the Temple. At the center of our story is our temple; that Temple we labor to erect in our hearts for the indwelling of God. Their story inspires us to, in the words of the Gospel of Matthew, "let your lights so shine before men, that they may see your good works, and glorify your Father which is in heaven." (Matt 5:16) I suppose, as Masons, we guard the routes to the East for those weary pilgrims traveling thereto in search of light.

Works Cited:

1) Coil, Henry Wilson, 33°. Coil's Masonic Encyclopedia. 1996, Richmond, VA: Macoy Publishing and Masonic Supply Co., Inc. Page 501.

2) Coil, page 499.

3) "Quietism," September 11, 2008, <http://en.wikipedia.org/wiki/Quietism_(Christian_philosophy)>.

4) Coil, page 499.

5) Coil, pages 501-502.

6) Coil, page 503.

7) Scottish Rite Journal. 2008.

8) Coil, page 349.

A SHORT HISTORY OF TABLE LODGES AND FESTIVE BOARDS IN FREEMASONRY

By: The Reverend Donald E. Brooks

The old saw that "the way to a man's heart is through his stomach" is probably true, as we men have from time immemorial, loved our food and beverage. Wherever the ancient lodges of Masons met, whether in the lean-to lodges attached to the buildings they were erecting, in the homes of the patrons of the various buildings they had come to build, or many other places, it seems that by the 16 and 1700's, the tavern or ale house became a favorite gathering place for lodge brothers to assemble, and there to have their meetings.

In England, prior to 1717, there were several lodges which met within the City of London and surrounds. Four of these, known as The Old Lodges, or Lodges of Time Immemorial, met in taverns for their regular communications: The Goose and Gridiron Ale House; The Crown Ale House, The Apple Tree Tavern, and The Rummer and Grapes Tavern. (1) In 1716, at a meeting in The Apple Tree Tavern, apparently on December 27, a decision was made to organize and constitute a Grand Lodge which would govern and stabilize the practice of speculative freemasonry in England, and would call the brethren back to the old practice of a quarterly conference and twice yearly observance of "The Feasts of the Craft." Such a gathering was held on June 24, 1717 at The Goose and Gridiron Ale House, and The English Grand Lodge of Freemasonry was constituted that day. (2)

It is easy to see today what the esoteric and philosophical reasons for these two specific feast days might have been. The summer feast marks the apogee of the sun to the zenith, and the longest day of the year. For a fraternity which uses light as a teaching symbol, and which in its inception was purely Christian, this day would be symbolically important. The winter feast marks what was or seemed the shortest day of the year, or the perigee of the sun's heavenly course, and prepared for the new dienatale Solus Invictus, the birthday of the Invincible Sun (or Son).

There is a suggestion by some historians that the call for a re-institution of the Annual Feast may have been the most important thing that the new Grand Lodge could have done. Not long after this call to revive the feast, Grand Master Sayers ordered that "the old, regular, and peculiar Toasts and Health's of Freemasons" be used at the banquet. (3) It is without doubt that either from the practice of holding the Great Feasts, along with their formal toasts and "healths," that the Table Lodge and Festive Boards arose, or that, as the brethren were already at table in an upstairs or otherwise secluded room in the tavern, that the rituals would be worked in that space. (4a)

One masonic historian notes, "In eighteenth century lodges, the feast bulked so large in the lodge that in many of them the members were seated at the table when the lodges were opened and remained at it throughout the Communication, even when the degrees were conferred." (4b)

What was the draw of the tavern and alehouse for the Mason of the day? While gentlemen of the day had their clubs and fine townhouses and estates to find solace from poverty and squalor, the public houses, inns, taverns and ale houses provided an opportunity for the common man to meet. There they could hear the latest news, shop-talk or gossip; eat a sumptuous meal of cheap meat, cheese and bread; and lift a beverage which would muddle the head and delight the heart. Here they would be provided a moment of gathered friendship and insulation from the ravages of 16th and 17th century England's daily grind. At the tavern, the publican could offer beyond the tasty food and frothy tankard, a relatively private room in which friends could gather to meet and discuss fraternal business of the day. (5)

Further, feasts were mentioned in minutes of several of the old lodges wherein the brethren would gather following an "entering" or "passing" of a man, and the lodge would gather about the "festive board" to honor both the brother initiated or passed, and to use the time to teach the work of the fraternity.

"The result," says masonic historian and writer H. L. Haywood, "was that Masonic fellowship was good fellowship in [the lodge], as in a warm and fruitful soil, acquaintanceship, friendship, and affection could flourish; there was no grim and silent sitting on a bench, staring across at a wall. Out of this festal spirit flowered the love which Masons had for their lodge. They brought gifts to it, and only by reading of old inventories can any present day Mason measure the extent of that love, there were gifts of chairs, tables, altars, pedestals, tapestries, draperies, silver, candle-sticks, oil paintings, libraries, Bibles, mementos, curios, regalia's and portraits. The lodge was a home, warm, comfortable, luxurious, full of memories, and tokens, and affection, and even if a member died, his presence was never wholly absent." (6)

It was clear that no one had to be reminded or even encouraged to go to lodge, for that was a haven of rest, relaxation, learning, enjoyment, and refreshment.

"What business has any lodge to be nothing but a machine for grinding out the work. It was not called into existence in order to have the minutes read. Even a mystic tie will snap under the strain of cheerlessness, repetition, monotony, dullness

A lodge needs a fire lighted in it, and the only way to have that warmth [was] to restore the lodge Feast, because when . . . restored, good fellowship and brotherly love will follow, and where good fellowship is, members will fill up an empty room not only with themselves but also with their gifts." (7)

Laurence Dermott, the well-known Grand Secretary of the Grand Lodge of the Ancients in England, (prior to the union of the two Grand Lodges) and author of Ahiman Rezon, the Constitutions of Masonry according the Grand Lodge of Ancient Freemasons, stated this in the mid 1700's about the Table Lodge:

"It was expedient to abolish the old custom of studying Geometry in the Lodge, and some younger Brethren made it appear that a good knife and fork, in the hands of a dexterous Brother, over proper Materials (food), would give great satisfaction and add more to the conviviality of the Lodge than the best Scale and Compasses in Europe." (8)

Clearly, this was an early introduction of the terms "Knife and Fork Mason" or the "Knife and Fork Degree" which we jokingly use today.

> *I do not attend the meetings*
> *for I've not the time to spare.*
> *But every time they have a feast*
> *you will surely find me there.*
> *I cannot help with the degrees*
> *for I do not know the work.*
> *But I can applaud the speakers,*
> *and handle a knife and fork.*
> *I'm so rusty in the ritual,*
> *it seems like Greek to me.*
> *But practice has made me perfect*
> *in the Knife and Fork Degree*
> *Brother Richard L. Kurtz (9)*

Table Lodges, as far as can be ascertained from rituals, minutes, etc., were organized in "peculiar" or specific orders and patterns which reflected the festive nature of the lodges. The lodges, being formed around and meeting at dining tables, conducted their meetings so that neither the ritual interfered with the serving, nor the serving with the ritual of the lodge. While hilarity and fun were enjoyed by the brethren, the esoteric as well as the common teachings of the fraternity were shared among the brethren.

The Table Lodge was apparently traditionally tiled as an Apprentice's Lodge, and followed a specially tailored or modified ritual, which would allow all Apprentices and Fellows to enter upon the enjoyment of the fellowship of the Lodge. (10) Brother Beresiner notes in his book 1723 and all that, ". . . since June 1717, Freemasons were doing pretty well, regularly meeting at taverns, dining and drinking whilst learning the ritual and conducting the ceremonies." (11)

One writer, in an introduction to Table Lodge protocol for his Grand Jurisdiction, suggests that in the fledgling United States, the Table Lodge was among the greatest assets of Masonry during the colonial period. With the political and economic problems of the day, the festivities, camaraderie and just pure individual and group support lifted the spirits of the Brothers of the Craft when times were at their worst. (12)

It is interesting to note at this point that while the facts to the story are sparse and tend to be vague, the traditional history of a severely shortened meeting of St Andrew's Lodge in Boston at a particular tavern suggest that lodge's major role in a famous "Tea Party" which may indeed have been planned over bread, cheese and ale at a Table Lodge by brothers in a particular Tavern in old Boston. (13)

A fitting fact, whether St. Andrew's Lodge helped to host a "Tea Party" following a Table Lodge or not, when Table Lodges are in session, traditionally the objects in the room take on a military "flavor." The Table becomes the "Trestleboard." Table cloths become "Standards," as in "flags." Plates are "tiles," dishes are "platforms," spoons are "trowels," knives are "swords," forks are "mattocks," and bottles become "barrels." The glasses used, especially certain glasses used for toasts, are called "canons." Please take time to look at the English Firing Glass I have brought today. Filling up the "canon" glasses is "to charge" the canon. Lights, particularly candles, are called "stars," chairs are "stalls," food is "materials," and bread is "Rough Ashlar." Red wine is "strong powder," water is "weak powder," salt and pepper are "sand" and "dust" respectively. To eat is to "masticate." To drink, following the term for the glass as a "canon," is "to Fire" or "Discharge" the canon. (14)

For any number of reasons, the room is arranged in a specific pattern, at least according to all but one of the rituals which this researcher has found. That separate ritual also gave the "usual" arrangement, with an alternative setup, but it was noted that the separate setup was to accommodate abnormally large groups. (15)

Normally, the tables are set up in an "open 'U' shape, with the Worshipful Master seated at the center or apex of the "U." The S W and the J W are seated at the far ends of the 'U' on the right and left respectively as one looks out from the apex. The brethren are seated on the outside of the 'U' with particular places assigned for the Chaplain, and other officers and special visitors. With this arrangement, the stewards or serving brothers will have ease of access to each dining brother, and whatever activity is in progress at the time of serving each course can proceed without interruption. If this is to be a Table Lodge rather than a "Festive Board" which is the hearty banquet following a tiled meeting in a lodge hall, and historically most often following a degree conferral, the Altar should be set up in the lower middle of the open 'U' in front of the WM, with the three G∴ L∴ around it as appropriate for the Jurisdiction in which it is being held.16

While the ceremonies for a Table Lodge as well as those for a formal Festive Board (which is generally functionally only differentiated by whether it is tiled and opened with the formal lodge ceremonial opening) are not well known among most Masons, the forms go back over three centuries in English, Scottish, Irish, and French Freemasonry. Twelve toasts or "Healths" were proposed in some of the rituals. Seven is the most usual number of toasts presently used. Following the proposal of a toast, except for certain ones which preclude such, a response is normally given by the honoree or a designee. Brother Yasha Beresiner, in one of his publications (Masonically Speaking: A Guide for Craft and other Speech Making; e-mailed excerpts from the author), notes a not uncommon situation which was true in the 1700's and is still true today:

The brother responding on behalf of the visitors had exceeded his allotted time and had the appearance of planning to goon for some time yet. The Master signaled his Warden with the gavel, implying that a gentle tap to the speaker's head may encourage him to sit down. The Warden, obedient to his Master's command crept behind the speaker, and as he was about to hit him, tripped and the gavel landed on the head of a brother sitting next to the speaker. Knocked semi-conscious, he slid under the table and was heard to say, "Hit me again! I can still hear him speak." (17)

The toasts and the proposers (according to one system) are:

1st *To the President of the United States*
2nd *To the Most Worshipful Grand Master and Most Worshipful Grand Lodge*
3rd *To the Worshipful Master of the Host Lodge*
4th *The Senior and Junior Wardens*
5th *To the Brethren in the Armed Forces*
6th *To the Other Officers and Visiting Brethren*
7th *To All Masons Wheresoever Dispersed Over the Face of the Globe (18)*

A second form is:

1st *To Our Country proposed by The WM*
2nd *To Our Gentle Craft proposed by the JD*
3rd *To Our Departed Brethren proposed by the Chap*
4th *To the Worshipful Master proposed by the SW*
5th *To the Grand Lodge proposed by the JW*
6th *To the Local Lodge (Name and #) proposed by a visiting WM or a local PM*
7th *To Our Visiting Brethren proposed by the SD*
8th *To the Initiate(s)/Passed Brother(s)/Raised Brother(s) proposed by a recent recipient*
9th *The Tiler's Toast (the LAST toast of the evening) by the Tiler. This toast is to all Masons where-so-ever spread over the face of the globe, and may be oriented toward "our absent brethren." There is never a response speaker to this one.*

Note that toasts '7' and '8' may be unnecessary on some evenings. The toasts may he specially composed far the evening, or one of the traditional prepared toasts may be used. The response by an appropriate Brother should not be over a few minutes in length, else the indented paragraph above might come into full "indenting" use. (19)

The seven toasts prescribed by the Grand Lodges of British Colombia, Iowa, and several other Grand Jurisdictions (with appropriate modifications) are very similar, follow old rituals, and provide an excellent framework for use in other Grand Jurisdictions. 1st the President of the United States; 2nd The Most Worshipful Grand Master and the Grand Lodge of your state; 3rd The Worshipful Master of the Host Lodge (and may include all present sitting Masters); 4th The Wardens of the Host Lodge (and may include all sitting Wardens); 5th Past Worshipful Master of the Host Lodge (and may include all visiting Past Masters), 6th All other Officers, new initiates and Visiting Brethren; 7th The Tiler's Toast to all Masons where-so-ever spread over the face of the globe and all absent Brethren. (20)

As an important note, the Grand Lodge of Tennessee prohibits the use of alcoholic beverages in masonic buildings and the use of such in any degree work except under certain well controlled conditions in certain rites which historically require small amounts to be used. Even then, alternatives must be provided for those who require it, or steps must be taken to allow the initiate/candidate to receive the ritualistic work without use of the beverage to the detriment of his health or conscience. While wine has been the beverage traditionally used in Table Lodges and at Festive Boards, other beverages can and should be used when there is any doubt as to the permissibility or appropriate of use of wine. Grape juice, cranberry juice, and of course, water (the elixir of life) are appropriate. (21)

As an important note, the Grand Lodge of Tennessee prohibits the use of alcoholic beverages in masonic buildings and the use of such in any degree work except under certain well controlled conditions in certain rites which historically require small amounts to be used. Even then, alternatives must be provided for those who require it, or steps must be taken to allow the initiate/candidate to receive the ritualistic work without use of the beverage to the detriment of his health or conscience. While wine has been the beverage traditionally used in Table Lodges and at Festive Boards, other beverages can and should be used when there is any doubt as to the permissibility or appropriate of use of wine. Grape juice, cranberry juice, and of course, water (the elixir of life) are appropriate. (21)

One of the rituals which has been consulted suggests a six course meal wherein the seven toasts are offered throughout the meal, and keeping the eating and toasting moving throughout the evening. The courses are suggested to allow for an adequate number of courses to fit the ceremonies, but to avoid creating a large, expensive, or difficult to prepare and serve meal. The courses suggested are, COURSE 1: (a) a small glass of an appetizer juice such as apple, cranberry or tomato, (b) a small wedge of cheese and two or three crackers, and (c) a few meatballs or cocktail sausages. With this course will come Toast 1. COURSE 2: (a) a small fruit salad, (b) a small sherbet, (c) a three bean salad. Toast 2. COURSE 3: (a) soup. Toast 3. COURSE 4: (a) fresh green garden salad with choice of dressing. Toast 4. COURSE 5: (a) Main Entree, such as braised chicken breast with steamed vegetables and rice, or sliced Beef Brisket with potato and vegetables. Toast 5. COURSE 6: (a) dessert. Toast 6. A speaker might be asked to make his presentation immediately after the dessert has been consumed. If there are only five courses, the first toast will commence the meal. Whichever way is chosen, the Seventh and last toast is the very last to come before the closing ritual or prayer, and traditionally is offered at or as close to 9:00 pm as possible. (22)

There are historically military "maneuvers" to be executed before and following each toast or "firing." While these may seem "silly" to some brothers, the system has been in use for more than three hundred years, and is a physical and kinetic connection to the actions, attitudes, and even beliefs of our more ancient brethren, just as the strange and sometimes less well understood words and actions of some of our degree ceremonies are equal connections with "antique masonry." According to "the orders for toasting" as put out by the Grand Lodge of Maine, adapted from one of the English systems, the Master, or whoever proposes the toast, following the statement of honor (to whom the toast is made), says, "Right hand to arms" when the members touch their right hands to the "firing" or wine glass. "Ready" at which the members raise the glass with outstretched arm. "Aim" at which the members bring the glass to their lips. "Fire, Good Fire, Fire All" where the members drink in three distinct motions.

"Present Arms" at which the members return the glass to the ready position. What follows is an interesting and very English maneuver. In quick time, the glass is carried to the left shoulder, the right shoulder, and to the outstretched position three times, then horizontally to the left, to the right, and to the table with some force, though not enough to shatter the glass. Note that the firing glasses are often specially made or engraved with the names and numbers of the lodges, and can be quite expensive. Following release of the glass, a battery of three times three follows with VIVAT said loudly three times.

There is also, in formal occasions, a "sword manual" which can follow using the table knives. Here the order is given "Advance Swords!" at which the brethren raise the table knife with the arm extended over the table. "Poise Swords!" at which the knife is elevated slightly. "Salute with Swords!" at which the handle of the knife touches the bearer's chin. "Swords at Rest!" at which the brethren strike the table with the knife. The same three times three battery is given followed by the same "VIVAT," which is tantamount to wishing long life to the brother saluted or toasted. (23)

Available online, from the publication divisions of several Grand Lodges, from various appendant Masonic Bodies in the United States, as well as from this researcher or, if I am so directed by the officers of this Lodge of Research, from its Secretary or other officer, is a compendium of different rituals from many Grand Jurisdictions and their related directions which can be used to set up either a "Table Lodge" (if it is approved by the Grand Master of the Jurisdiction) or for a Festive Board following a Masonic Communication. Many of the ritualistic items, while similar in some ways to actual Masonic Ceremonies in opening, closing, or conferring degrees, could be slightly adapted, should the lodge so desire, to be used with profanes and lady guests present. I have attended at least one such "Ceremonial and Catered Festive Boards" here in Tennessee.

This last statement brings me to the crux of this paper. I have, over my thirty-eight years of being a Mason, had the pleasure of being welcomed into the Scottish Grand Lodge Hall, and the Scottish Grand Chapter/ Council and Great Royal Order of Scotland Hall. I have been welcomed into the halls of The United Grand Lodge of England and of various English Lodges. I have been queried and welcomed into many Grand and Subordinate or Constituent Lodges across the United States. To witness the ceremonies and rituals, the regalia and the furniture of these lodges, to see and hear the "Living History" of the brotherhood has been exciting and wonderful. But to witness and get to know and celebrate the fraternity and the reality of brotherhood brother to brother over a table with food and beverage, has been most rewarding of all.

I wish to quote a few lines from Brother Yasha Beresiner, who has been cited previously in this paper. Brother Beresiner is a noted writer in London, a guide to London's points of interest, a brother Mason, and a close friend of one of my first met English Brothers, Brother Christopher Nicholls, PM, and currently Secretary of Coopers Old Boys Lodge #5211, my own lodge by "British Honour" in London, England.

"When you browse through the history of our remarkable craft," says Brother Beresiner, *"you will find it impossible to get away from eating, drinking, food and speeches from the very start. After all, organized Freemasonry began in June 1717 around a dining table at the Goose and Gridiron in London, and seven decades earlier, in the early evening of the 16th October, 1646, Elias Ashmole wined and dined, following his initiation in Warrington (his father-in-law's home)."* (Note received by e-mail) *"The majority of lodges have always had some refreshment after their meetings. Outside of London in the 18th and 19th centuries where the brethren would have had some distance to travel, meetings were held during the day or as near to the full moon as possible....The repast in an ordinary Provincial Lodge would have been informal in the 1800's. Extant records give the menu: cottage loaves, cheese, pickled onions and large quantities of beer in a warm and friendly ambience. London, the metropolis that it was by Victorian times, had a greater concentration of lodges and Masons and held far more elaborate dinners. The fact that the Victorian middle classes were big eaters is reflected in the surviving menus, especially of Installation and Consecration meetings. It would not be unusual to have a menu with ten courses, giving alternative choices for many of the dishes and a selection of wines and liqueurs to assist with digestion. Music was very much part of the Masonic dinner scene of the period. Anderson, in his first Constitutions, encouraged it by publishing words and music for the benefit of the brethren. Available [written] records of the mid-1700's show members of the lodge singing to the accompaniment of a violin or flute. Towards the end of the century and start of the nineteenth in London and other large cities such as Manchester and Birmingham, well-known professional performers, string quartets, solo violinists, cellists, and male and female vocalists, were hired to entertain the brethren. They all offered their services in contemporary advertisements published in the Masonic press."* (24)

While the Table Lodge (and Festive Board) are certainly part of our fraternal history, this writer is convinced that these are items which deserve our attention again. Smaller lodges, and sometimes some of the larger ones have given up on such an activity as the regular festive board before or for preferable reasons including assuring that brethren do not leave before the enjoyment of the feast begins, after meetings or the occasional Ceremonial Banquet because of time or effort.

Some have given up because brothers want to have a short and cursory "just read-the-minutes meeting" and go home, with no time for banter, boiled beef, beverage OR brotherhood. These are also often the lodges whose membership is dwindling, and the lodges and brethren who wonder how long they will be able to remain viable lodges. When we are able to find methods of increasing the camaraderie and interest in our members, to get them intrigued as to what the evening's monthly program might be, and who might be visiting, the joy of lifted spirits in dining together, and the exciting sharing of old times and new friends and brothers, this researcher believes we will find new life and excitement among the ranks of the members of Our Gentle Craft, and within our Lodges. The writer of the article on "Table Lodge History and Ritual" for Phoenix masonry Incorporated, states: "The Table Lodge is the summary of Masonic Doctrine. It prescribes reverence for Divinity and the Moral Law. It strengthens the devotion that Masons hold for the Lodge and Country. It increases the unity and fellowship of the Craft."25

Brethren, Feed the Mind, Feed the Body, Feed the Soul....Feed and Grow Masonry!

WORKING BIBLIOGRAPHY

1) Chandler, Glenn E., Jr., "The Four Old Lodges," Internet published paper presented to Wilbur W. Masters, Jr. Council No. 322 AMD, 4-29-2004.

2) ibid.

3) Grand Lodge of Maine, Ancient Free & Accepted Masons, "Guidelines for Table Lodge", no author cited. http://www.mainemason.org/resources/table.asp.

4a & 4b) Grand Lodge of Main, loc cit.

5) Masters, Wilber W.,Loc cit.

6) Grand Lodge of Maine,loc cit.
7) Grand Lodge of Maine, page 2.

8) "The Table Lodge: A History", http://www.phoenixmasonry.org/table_lodge_history_ritual.htm, Page 2

9) *Beresiner, Yasha.Masonically Speaking: A Guide, for Craft and other Speech Making, frompage 3 of the notes emailed to me and used by permission of the author.*

10) "The Table Lodge: A History", page 2.

11) Beresiner, page 2 of emailed notes.

12) "The Table Lodge:A History", page 2.

13) A well-known common story which may or may not have historic validity.

14) "The Table Lodge: A History", page 2.

15) Grand Lodge of Maine, page 2.

16) ibid, pages 3 and 4.

17) Beresiner, ("Refreshment" section), page 1 of notes.

18) Grand Lodge of Maine, page 2.

19) Burbank (CA) Masonic Lodge No. 406 F. & A.M. "A Masonic Table Lodge", http://www.calodges-org/no406/TABLE98-HTM.

20) "How to conduct a table lodge",The Masonic Service Committee, Grand Lodge of Iowa, A. F. & A M 1941, through the Website of the Grand Lodge of British Columbia, http://freemasonry.bcy.ca/texts/tablelodge.html, pages 1-3.

21) "Tennessee Masonic Code".

22) "The Table Lodge: A History", pages 4-5.

23) Grand Lodge of Maine, pages 4-5.

24) Beresiner, ("Introduction" section), page 1 and ("Entertainment" section), page 2 of notes.

25) "The Table Lodge: A History", pages 4-5.

THE MASONIC HEART

By Thomas J. Driber

The number of Masons who have traditionally entered the Lodge on an impulse must be few, as impulses are generally not long lasting and the Initiation, Passing, and Raising is necessarily protracted according to the Lunar Cycle and among other things, serve to offset any impulsive petitions that are not heartfelt. Occasionally, despite our best effort and the impediments of design, there are a few who pass the West Gate that should not, but the true Mason could not avoid finding his way to the door of the Lodge. In some ways it may, for many, seem pre-destined.

Although most have given considerable thought to knocking at the door of Masonry it is more than linear thought that drives a Brother to find his way.

Where was he first prepared? Long before he submitted a petition he felt moved in his heart. He was there, first prepared! A variety of different prods may have stimulated his cognitive awareness of Masonry, but it was a positive heart-felt feeling that led to his linear good opinion of the Craft. It's his heart-felt fidelity that keeps him returning and progressing in moral science.

Too often since the Age of Reason we are propelled to cerebral analysis in the perpetual gathering of material goods, status, and acclaim, while anything resembling feelings has been dismissed as "soft", "fuzzy", "high risk", "sentimental", and "unreliable". Feelings are not "cool". They portray vulnerability and weakness. So, we think and fail to feel, yet in our first preparation it seems we both thought and felt something about Masonry. And, on that basis did we choose to petition, and on that basis have we each progressed in the art and science of Freemasonry.

"The heart has long been considered the seat of our emotions. The Mesopotamians, Egyptians, Babylonians, and Grecian culture all recognized the heart as the organ directing emotions, morality, and decision making." Proverbs 23:7 tells us that, "as a man thinks in his heart, so is he." In Luke 5:22 he asks, "what reason you in your hearts?" In mystical Judaism the heart energy center is responsible for "Beauty, Harmony, and Balance," all qualities well known to Freemasons. The "Judaic heart" is the key to health and well being. Many Yogic systems recognize the heart as the core of human consciousness. Chinese medicine has for many centuries held that the connecting pathway between the body and the mind is the heart and through its pulsations are read the pathologies affecting a patient's wellness and balance. In Japan shinzu denotes the heart muscle while kokoro is used to express the concept of the "mind of the heart."

Amongst all these notions is the common thread that the heart is a center of an independent intelligence capable of independent decision yet working in coordinated communication with the linear decision making brain. (1)

Our deepest secrets are safely deposited within our breast. We vow to keep a Brother's secrets as safe and inviolable within our breast as within his own and we might then construe that within our hearts are kept our inmost thoughts and feelings. We use phrases such as "with all our heart", or "having our heart set on ..." as common idioms today. (2) Linear science has for the most part dismissed such references as folksy wisdom without much in the way of empirical value and defiant of measurement parameters. Science has had little interest in the reservoir of knowledge contained within the Masonic corpus yet it would now seem that a body of scientific experimentation and reported findings lend support to being first prepared in one's heart. The ancient wisdom known across time and cultures now seems to find common ground in the marriage of the heart as an anatomical/physiological organ and the heart as a source of decision making intelligence.

The Institute of Heart Math (IHM) in California has pioneered new research into the intelligence of the heart. Their research is widely published in respected texts and traditional scientific and medical journals and has produced a thoroughly new understanding of the heart and its interrelatedness to the brain and other organs. They have shown in scientific terms why we can now understand why we were first prepared for Masonry in our hearts.

By measuring the electrical activity of the heart IHM has shown that the heart is the largest waveform generator of the human body. It's capable of entraining the electrical waveforms of the brain, the immune system and other systems of the body. Entrainment is best understood as a physics phenomenon of resonance that was first observed in 1665 by Dutch Scientist Christian Huygens while working on the design of the pendulum clock. Huygen noticed that two pendulum clocks with the pendulums swinging at different rates eventually ended up swinging in unison at the same rate due to their mutual influence on one another. From his observation entrainment is defined as the tendency for two oscillating bodies to lock into phase so that they vibrate in harmony, or simply the synchronizing of two or more rhythmic cycles. With respect to heart muscle cells, when two or more are brought into close proximity the cells will pulsate in synchrony. (3)

IHM has also recorded the effect of heart pulsation in the electrical recording of the brain. Even further, they have recorded the heart beat of one person in the brain waves of another while both subjects were simultaneously shaking hands with each other (4) yielding yet a whole new meaning to the modes of recognition amongst Brothers.

Additionally, IHM has recorded an electromagnetic field generated specifically by the heart that is in addition to that electromagnetic field previously shown as the human aura, also known as prana in the ancient Sanskrit. This field of electromagnetic energy exists in a configuration known as a torus and has been measured extending eight feet out from the body itself (5).

According to Childre the heart has its own intelligence and consciousness. "It has unusual perceptual and intuitive information-processing capabilities; its frequency range of intelligence is not controlled by the brain nor by the autonomic nervous system; it is auto-rhythmic, beating on its own without requiring input from the brain or nervous system although both communicate with each other through neural and hormonal pathways directly affecting perception, reaction times, intuition, and decision making ability." Feelings and emotions experienced by the heart are communicated directly to the brain via neurotransmitters and hormones which create chemical changes throughout the organ systems of the entire body (6).

Moreover, the heart has an effect on the immune system, DHEA production, DNA, cell growth, and tumor inhibition when coherent emotion is intentionally created by using "specially designed mental and emotion self management techniques which involve intentionally quieting the mind, shifting one's awareness to the heart area, and focusing on positive emotions" (7)

Harris cites Vincent Giampapa, MD, who has found that subjects in a relaxed state (coherent) can directly access their own DNA and effectively reverse the signs of ageing. Coupling a relaxed state with binaural beat technology, Giampapa reported a 46 % decrease in blood Cortisol levels, a 97% Melatonin increase and a 43% increase in blood DHEA levels. It is of some significance that Giampapa found that by increasing DHEA levels by 100 micrograms/deciliter of blood, mortality from cardiovascular disease decreased by 48%. (8) It may then be possible for nearly half of the brethren to eliminate some degree of cardiovascular risk simply by renewing coherent core emotions in their heart that were the basis of the first preparation, albeit unknown at the time.

Adding to the body of new science in understanding the heart is the work done in quantum biology where research findings suggest that our DNA has a phantom effect with that which it has ever had contact. Poponin and Gariaev demonstrated the effect of human DNA on the arrangement of photons (light particles) contained within a glass vacuum. In a glass vacuum without the presence of human DNA, photons were observed in scattered random array. Following the introduction of human DNA into the vacuum environment the photons arranged themselves in an organized way. When the DNA was removed the photons retained their ordered arrangement suggesting that the stuff of which we're made has a direct affect on the quantum building blocks that make up our world (9).

48

Other research scientists working with U.S. Army personnel sought to determine the effect of human feelings on human DNA when the DNA was separated from the subject. Traditionally, we would readily recognize that no such effect could exist once the DNA tissue was separated from its donor. In fact, human DNA responded by relaxing and contracting its helix according to the kind of emotion evoked in the donor. The effect was observed even at a distance of 500 miles in separation between the DNA tissue samples and the donors, and the key to the DNA responsiveness was genuine feelings of emotion(10) (11).

When we put the scientific findings into a practical perspective it seems that there is indeed something to the idea of heart intelligence beyond just the mushy sentimentality that would have been used to explain the answer to the question; "Where were you first prepared". It seems evident that our DNA has a direct effect on the quanta, the photon particles of light that make up our world. Whether our DNA is still attached to our bodies or separated by mere walls or hundreds of miles there remains some manner of molecular connection where the effect remains the same. The Institute of Heart Math has shown beyond doubt that a principal factor in affecting our DNA and the quantum world around us is our own core heart emotions.

Now, can a case be made for a cause and effect relationship between the new discoveries of quantum physics, quantum biology, neural technologies, neurotransmitter blood levels and a core heart feeling that leads one to contemplate Freemasonry, become a Freemason, and actually put into practice the tenets of a moral science? If Masonry is based on brotherly love, relief, and truth it would seem possible. If the Masonic principles are based on pure morality; if its sentiments are those of an exalted benevolence; if it supports all that is good, and kind, and charitable it would then seem that Masonry provides an inexhaustible supply of opportunity for positive core heart feelings that could prompt any petitioner to proceed forward. But, was the question posed in the catechetical lecture with purposeful intent in the first place? If so, it suggests that those who composed the rituals had some level of insight into quantum theory way back there in the middle Ages. That seems unlikely!

A. E. Waite, in discussing Masonic links to the chivalric Order of the Temple, says that the Templar Knights were the prototype of Masonry as they erected their temple within their heart first. Why? Waite further describes his belief that Craft Masonry has been symbolic of a secret tradition that has its roots in a Secret Doctrine of Israel and that those who composed the rituals knew of this secret doctrine and that the Masonic ritual is the most sublime evidence ever put into the written form (12).

Although not explicitly stated and certainly more esoterically expansive than this one particular variation on the Masonic theme, the secret doctrine may simply have been, in part, an awareness of the importance of combining positive core heart emotions (IHM) with linear thought in order to achieve a meaningful understanding of the mystical component of their temporal mortality.

In their text The Spiritual Anatomy of Emotion (to be released July 2009), Jawer and Micozzi contend that emotion is the greatest influence on personality and that further, emotion plays a key role in immunity, stress, cognition, sensation, and emotional expression even with regard to psychosomatic illness (13).

Daniels and Daniels in Matrix Meditations (to be released in August 2009), offer a sixteen week program for the development of a heart-mind connection using various meditative techniques from both Eastern and Western spiritual traditions where concentration, contemplation, mindfulness, and awareness are the key forms to achieving mental clarity, expanding creative thought, and modifying behavior (14).

In conclusion it seems that there is a universal and time enduring notion that is now better defined as a scientific paradigm, that we are able to achieve more than dry, mundane, purely objective decision making by accessing the emotional feeling centers within the heart, and coupling those emotions with our ability to think in linear terms. This has been long known in Freemasonry, but probably little understood and taken simply as a matter of sentimental form, if even that. And so, the question and answer of where a Mason is first prepared to be a Mason gains support from new science and ongoing research that even further suggests that our DNA is the "software" through which we can renew not only our bodies but actuate, with coupled core heart emotions including love, compassion, forgiveness, and gratitude, all that is good, and kind, and charitable as we go about erecting that "house not made with hands, eternal in the heavens" and while simultaneously pursuing our own super-longevity (15).

Bibliography:

1) Childre, D., Martin, H., with Beech, D., The HeartMath Solution, p.8, Harper SanFrancisco, 1999.

2) Brandon, D., "Heart Centeredness", Inner Change Magazine, April-May, 1997.

3) Website; Soundfeelings@http://www.soundfeelings.com "The Entrainment Principle"

4) Childre, D., Martin, H., with Beech, D. The Heartmath Solution, pp.38-41, HarperSanFrancisco, 1999

5) Braden, G., The Divine Matrix, Hay House, Inc., p.51, Carlsbad, CA and New York City 2007.

6) Childre, D., IHM, "A White Paper: Women Lead with Their Hearts" quoted by Brandon, D. in "Heart Centeredness", 1997.

7) Rein, G., McCraty, R., "Structural Changes in Water and DNA Associated with New Physiologically Measurable States", Journal of Scientific Exploration, vol. 8, # 3, pp. 438-439, 1994.

8) Harris, B. "The Science Behind Holosync and Other Neuraltechnologies Using Binaural Beats", Centerpointe Research Institute, Beaverton, OR. www.Holosync.com 2008.

9) Poponin, V., "The DNA Phantom Effect: Direct Measurement of a New Field in Vacuum Substructure", www.twm.co.nz/DNAphantom.htm 2002.

10) Motz, J., "Everyone an Energy Healer: The Treat V Conference", Santa Fe, NM, in Advances: Journal of Mind-Body Health, vol. 9, 1993.

11) Rein, G., et al, "The Physiological and Psychological Effects of Compassion and Anger", Journal of Advancement in Medicine, vol. 8, #2, pp. 87-103, 1995.

12) Waite, A.E., The Secret Traditions of Freemasonry, Rebmon, London, England, 1911, as part of a discussion in The Secrets of Freemasonry, Lomas, R., pp 253-255, Magpie Books, London, England, 2006.

13) Jawer, M.A., Micozzi, M.S. The Spiritual Anatomy of Emotion, Park Street Press, as pre-publication summary discussion found in Inner Traditions Bear & Company, Rochester, VT, 2009.

14) Daniels, V., Daniels, K. N., Matrix Meditations, Destiny Books, as a pre-publication summary discussion found in Inner Traditions Bear & company, Rochester, VT, 2009.

15) Giampapa, V., "Super-Longevity", a binaural beat audio program of Holosync Technology, Centerpointe Research Institute, Beaverton, OR, 2008.

CORN, WINE, OIL, AND ANCIENT ISRAEL

By George C. Ladd III

Since I was raised to the sublime degree of Master Mason seven and a half years ago, I have never ceased to be amazed at Masonry's ability to appear at unexpected times (especially in Church), or in the most unexpected places. I was blessed this year to take a tour of Israel. At the very first activity on our tour immediately following our arrival at the Tel Aviv Airport, I was treated to a lecture on corn, wine, and oil.

We were taken via our tour bus from the airport to sort of national park called Ne'ot Kedumim—the Biblical Land Preserve, located between Tel Aviv and Jerusalem. Here they endeavor "to re-create the physical setting of the Bible in all its depth and detail. . . ." In their own words from their website "The Bible conveys its ideas not in abstract terms, but through a clear and vivid record of long human interaction with the land of Israel. Neot Kedumim draws on a variety of disciplines—such as Bible scholarship, botany, zoology, geography, history, and archaeology—to bring the Bible and its commentaries to life. Neot Kedumim has constructed a network of natural and agricultural landscapes bearing names that indicate their textual source:

- the Forest of Milk and Honey
- the Dale of the Song of Songs
- Isaiah's Vineyard
- the Fields of the Seven Varieties
- and many more.

"Thousands of tons of soil were trucked in and spread on the eroded hillsides, reservoirs were dug to catch runoff rainwater, and ancient terraces were restored. Habitats were created for such varied species as cedars from the snow-covered mountains of Lebanon and date palms from Sinai desert oases."

"Hundreds of varieties of biblical and talmudic plants; wild and domesticated animals; ancient and reconstructed olive and wine presses, threshing floors, cisterns, and ritual baths bring to life the literal roots of the biblical tradition in the soil of the land of Israel." (1)

We were given a tour of this park by a lady who is sort of a park ranger and interpreter, and were shown various plants, agricultural fields, and animals. She explained how each of these were mentioned in or were a part of the Bible. Early on, she explained to us about Corn, Wine, and Oil.

"I will respond, declares the Lord. I will respond to the heavens, and they will respond to the earth, and the earth shall respond with grain, with wine, and with oil" (Hosea 2:23-24).

As the virtual tour from Ne'ot Kedumim's website states, "It is this trio (grain, wine, and oil) that, throughout the Bible, represents the divine response, through the heavens, to the earth, and, through the earth, to human needs. God speaks to people through the seasonal rain from the heavens, vital for these three crops: 'If you obey the commandments that I enjoin upon you this day, loving the Lord your God and serving Him with all your heart and soul, I will grant the rain for your land in season, the early rain and the late, and you shall gather in your grain and your wine and your oil.' (Deuteronomy 11:13 - 14) With the "rain in season," grain (wheat), wine (grapes) & oil (olives) flourish in Israel's dry, rocky soil. Wheat, grapes, and olives became the staple products of ancient Israel. (2)

Deuteronomy, Chapter 7, Verses 12 and 13 state "And because you hearken to these ordinances, and keep and do them, the Lord your God will keep with you the covenant and the steadfast love which he swore to your fathers to keep; he will love you, bless you, and multiply you; he will also bless the fruit of your body and the fruit of your ground, your grain and your wine and your oil, the increase of your cattle and the young of your flock, in the land which he swore to your fathers to give you.

Corn, of course, is used in the British sense of that word to mean wheat, and not maize, which is what we Americans usually mean when we use the word, "corn." The Talmud lists 11 tasks associated with growing and harvesting wheat, "to bring forth bread from the earth." These are "plow, sow, reap, bind the sheaves, thresh, winnow, sieve, grind the grain, sift the flour, knead, bake."

It is no coincidence that grain is first in the list of grain, wine, and oil. Wheat was the queen of the crops. The ancient Israelite got 50 percent of his calories from wheat, mostly in the form of bread. Lehem, bread in Hebrew, is also the generic word for food. Bread is still the central food in Jewish religious life. Blessing the bread blesses the entire meal, and eating bread requires the ritual hand-washing before and the grace after. (3)

But wheat—life—is highly dependent on the "rain in season, the early rain and the late"—the first rains for the seed to germinate, the last for the kernels to ripen and fill with starch. If the farmer's prayers have been answered—if the rains come on time …then "those who sow in tears will reap with songs of joy" (Psalm 126:5). (4)

Wine, it turns out, was essential to a person's fluid intake in ancient Israel. Other than the region along the River Jordan and the occasional oasis, Israel, largely a desert country, had one source for water—rain. The Hebrew words for heaven, shamayim, and water, mayim, share the same root. Etymologically, in Hebrew, water comes from heaven. Rain is Israel's "only major source of water, and the rain comes, at most, six months of the year. How did people survive the dry months? Cisterns. Hewed laboriously out of solid rock, the cistern functions as a bank. You deposit every drop in the winter, and withdraw, very, very carefully, during the summer." During our tour, one of the main features of every ancient city or town that we saw was a large cistern.

One generally does not drink this stagnant cistern water by itself. It had to be mixed with wine to disinfect it. Hence, one's fluid intake consisted solely of wine, or of wine mixed with water.

According to Ne'ot Kedumim's website, "In the ancient Mediterranean, wine was an important component of the diet and a major source of calories, sugar, and iron. In ancient Israel, the drinking water available at the end of the summer was rainwater that had been sitting in a cistern for at least six months. Adding wine to the water improved the taste and lowered the bacteria content. Water mixed with wine was a standard drink. And "wine gladdens the human heart" (Psalm 104:15). Every holiday, every family celebration, is sanctified by blessing the fruit of the vine." (5)

Grapes grow throughout Israel. In the early spring, the leaves and delicate white flowers appear on the vines, and the fruit ripens in mid- to late summer. To harvest the grapes quickly before they spoil on the vine, the entire family moves into the vineyard watchtower, to harvest, tread the grapes in the winepress, and store the fresh juice in jugs to ferment.

Like wheat, grapes depend on the winter rains. Without enough water during the winter, the growing parts of the vine shrivel. But the same rain that can benefit the wheat in the spring can damage the grapes if the blossoms have already opened. And the heat that the grape blossoms need to open and be pollinated can parch the wheat. A tricky situation. (6)

Oil is olive oil. I suppose my first thought when I think of oil is anointing. But olive oil had a variety of uses in ancient Israel, the primary one being light from clay oil lamps. These were the light-bulbs of ancient Israel. Olive trees can live for a thousand years and bear fruit for centuries. Olive oil is one of the blessings of the land, highly valued for cooking, healing, and especially for lighting. "Messiah" is the Hebrew mashiakh—the one who is anointed—with olive oil. (7)

The green olives are harvested in the fall, and the ripe, black olives, full of oil, in November and December. To make oil, the olives are first crushed by a large, rotating stone. The olive pulp is then put in round, woven baskets and the oil is squeezed out. (8) Like the grapes, olives bloom in the spring. The delicate olive flowers are in the same vulnerable state as the grape blossoms, easily damaged by the winds and the late rains of April. (9)

In order to survive, the ancient Israelite needed all three—the grain and the wine and the oil. For the wheat and the grapes and the olives to all grow, a fine-tuned ecological balance was needed—a balance between rain and sun, heat and cold, that was—and is—beyond human control. (10) For this life-sustaining balance, the ancient Israelite farmer could only hope—and pray. Inevitably, the grain, the wine, and the oil became major players in his ritual life. The Temple ritual centered on a permanent display of twelve loaves—the showbread—and the menorah that was lit with olive oil. A wine libation was poured over the altar. The grain offering was semolina from the inner kernel of the wheat mixed with olive oil.

In the course of history, the Temple was destroyed, and with it the powerful rituals that channeled and focused the plea for survival. The Jews scattered from Israel to every corner of the earth.11 But the grain, the wine, and the oil were not forgotten. How is every Jewish holiday, every Sabbath, sanctified? By blessing bread, and blessing wine, and kindling lights. The Sabbath table, no matter where in the world, holds a weekly reminder of the ancient Jewish origins in a narrow, rocky strip of East Mediterranean coast, of the ancient Israelite farmer's fervent plea for the ecological balance that meant survival, and of our own ultimate dependence on the earth. (12)

Thus, corn, wine, and oil represent the essentials for human existence: food, liquids, light. (13)

I was immediately struck by the association of oil with light, which I had not perceived before. When I considered the wages of a Fellowcraft Mason, I immediately saw a relationship between the activities of the Fellowcraft and the procurement of more light. The Fellowcraft is to come out of ignorance into knowledge. His wages supply him with nourishment, refreshment, and more light. A major source of light is his cultivation of the seven liberal arts and sciences. Manly P. Hall asserted that "Equipped with the knowledge conferred by familiarity with the liberal arts and sciences, the studious Freemason therefore finds himself confronted by few problems with which he cannot cope." (14) These arts and sciences are the means by which we "trace the power, wisdom, and goodness of the Grand Artificer of the Universe," being the means by which we "minutely analyze his works."

I urge you to read Dr. Philip Phillips' paper, "The Seven Liberal Arts in the Fellowcraft Degree," printed in the Tennessee Lodge of Research's book, Traveling East, on pages 400-410.15

For a Masonic Treatment of Corn, Wine, and Oil, I recommend Short Talks Bulletin from August 1930, which treats the subject of corn, wine, and oil very well from the point of view of Masonry (reprinted following this article).16

For an esoteric exploration of the possible meanings of Corn, Wine, and Oil, see Dr. Thomas Driber's paper, "The Secrets of the Fellowcraft Degree," in Traveling East on pages 193-209.17

Works Cited

1) *"What Are We," June 13, 2008, <http://www.n-k.org.il/public/english/what/what.htm>.*

2) *"GRAIN, WINE, AND OIL - virtual tour at Neot-Kedumim," June 13, 2008, <http://www.n-k.org.il/public/english/what/v_tours/gwo/gwo_2.htm>.*

3) *"GRAIN, WINE, AND OIL - virtual tour at Neot-Kedumim," June 13, 2008, <http://www.n-k.org.il/public/english/what/v_tours/gwo/gwo_3.htm>.*

4) *"GRAIN, WINE, AND OIL - virtual tour at Neot-Kedumim," June 13, 2008, <http://www.n-k.org.il/public/english/what/v_tours/gwo/gwo_5.htm>.*

5) *"GRAIN, WINE, AND OIL - virtual tour at Neot-Kedumim," June 13, 2008, <http://www.n-k.org.il/public/english/what/v_tours/gwo/gwo_6.htm>.*

6) *"GRAIN, WINE, AND OIL - virtual tour at Neot-Kedumim," June 13, 2008, <http://www.n-k.org.il/public/english/what/v_tours/gwo/gwo_7.htm>.*

7) *"GRAIN, WINE, AND OIL - virtual tour at Neot-Kedumim," June 13, 2008, <http://www.n-k.org.il/public/english/what/v_tours/gwo/gwo_8.htm>.*

8) *"GRAIN, WINE, AND OIL - virtual tour at Neot-Kedumim," June 13, 2008,*

<http://www.n-k.org.il/public/english/what/v_tours/gwo/gwo_9. htm>.

9) *"GRAIN, WINE, AND OIL - virtual tour at Neot-Kedumim," June 13, 2008, <http://www.n-k.org.il/public/english/what/v_tours/gwo/gwo_10. htm>.*

10) *"GRAIN, WINE, AND OIL - virtual tour at Neot-Kedumim," June 13, 2008, <http://www.n-k.org.il/public/english/what/v_tours/gwo/ gwo_11.htm>.*

11) *"GRAIN, WINE, AND OIL - virtual tour at Neot-Kedumim," June 13, 2008, <http://www.n-k.org.il/public/english/what/v_tours/gwo/ gwo_12.htm>.*

12) *"GRAIN, WINE, AND OIL - virtual tour at Neot-Kedumim," June 13, 2008, <http://www.n-k.org.il/public/english/what/v_tours/gwo/ gwo_13.htm>.*

13) *"Hands-on Installations - Neot Kedumim The Biblical Landscape Reserve in Israel," June 13, 2008, <http://www.n-k.org. il/public/english/what/hans_on/hands_on.htm>.*

14) *Hall, Manly P., The Secret Teachings of All Ages (Los Angeles: Philosopical Research Society, 1975) 173-174.*

15) *Driber, Thomas J., Ph.D. and Philip E. Phillips, Ph.D., Traveling East. (Nashville: Eveready Press, 2006) 400-410.*

16) *The Short Talk Bulletin, The Masonic Service Association of the United States, VOL. 8 AUGUST 1930 NO. 8.*

17) *Driber, Thomas J., Ph.D. and Philip E. Phillips, Ph.D., Traveling East. (Nashville: Eveready Press, 2006) 193-209.*

THE INEFFABLE NAME ENCRYPTED IN THE INEFFABLE DEGREES

By Thomas J. Driber

The Ineffable Name is the Ineffable Word, the Incommunicable Name expressed for us in the Tetragrammaton as the symbolic word expressed in four letters which denote the name of God and which always applies to the Hebrew word only (Mackey 1882).

In this regard Albert Pike says, "Every degree of the Order has a Word which expresses its meaning. There is for Hiram only one Word, but this is pronounced in three different manners. There is one for the Apprentices . . . another for the Fellow-crafts . . . and another for the Masters; and in their mouth it signifies Truth, a word that is explained by Wisdom. This Word is that used to designate God, whose true name is ineffable and incommunicable" (Pike 1956).

Whilst at the Burning Bush this name, as indicated in the Book of Exodus, was communicated to Moses, "Thus shalt thou say unto the children of Israel: Jehovah, the God of your fathers, the God of Abraham, the God of Isaac, and the God of Jacob, hath sent me to you: this is my name forever, and this is my memorial unto all generations." (Exodus)

And again in Exodus Chapter VI: "I am Jehovah; and I appeared unto Abraham, unto Isaac, and unto Jacob, by the name El Shaddai; but by my name Jehovah was I not known unto them" (Exodus).

Although we venture the pronunciation of this Name of God, there is no authoritative agreement as to the proper pronunciation, although it is variously accepted as Yahweh or Jehovah or Yehavah as in the less familiar Yehavah Al Alohim and "which is rendered Lord-God" (Hutchens 2006). Irrespective of vowel differentiations each has the same numerical value when transliterated from alpha characters to numerical equivalents. The sum of the numerical value of each consonant in the Ineffable Name is 26. It is variously written in Masonry as the Hebrew letter Yod, equivalent to the English letters I, or J, or Y, and often enclosed within an equilateral triangle; He, equivalent to the letter H; Vauv, equivalent to the letter V or W; and concluded with the letter He or H again. The Hebrew numerical equivalent of Y is 10. The numerical equivalent of the letter He or H is 5 and the numerical equivalent of Vauv, V or W is 6. We find it written also in Phoenician characters as upon the jewel in the 14th Degree (Hutchens 1995).

Because Masonry speaks to us in a language of symbols we must be cognizant of the Ineffable Name expressed not only in Hebrew and Phoenician letters but also through numbers and other symbols. It is the intent herein to identify some of the more common, yet cryptic forms of the Ineffable Name in each of the ten Degrees of Perfection. In review of the 4th Degree it is said that "the AGE of a Secret Master is nine years (Pike 1982). Insomuch as the word "age" is fully capitalized in the text it is a hint to us that we think beyond the mere number of years. In this context the term AGE must mean something more.

If we think of the number 9 as the square of 3 it begins to take on different connotations. Imagine one square containing nine smaller squares within it and each smaller square containing a different digit comprised of 1 through 9. By placing those nine digits in a specific order we will configure the well known Pythagorean Talisman shown here:

8	1	6
3	5	7
4	9	2

Ill. 1, Pythagorean Talisman

The Talisman is significant because in each row, in each column and from corner to corner the numbers are summed to the number 15. This is of significance in understanding Masonry when we separate the number 15 into two of its components. Thus we will have a number 10 and a number 5. By transliterating 10 to the Hebrew letter equivalent we get the letter Yod or Y. Doing likewise with the number 5 we would transliterate to the letter He or H thus yielding the first two letters of the Ineffable Name YH and commensurate with either YAH, JAH, or YEH as symbolic of the Sacred Name (Mackey 1882).

It is also noted that Hebrew letters as well as Arabic letters are primarily consonants and a few of them are used secondarily to represent vowels, but full indication of vowels, when provided at all, is by means of a system of dots or strokes adjacent to the consonant characters (Webster's 1981). None of which is allowed by the Pythagorean Talisman. We are, therefore, left to choose vowels at our leisure.

It is also quickly recognized that the middle row of numbers is 3-5-7, the same as the steps of the Winding Stairs to the Middle Chamber which Mackey claims is symbolic of this life and which approximates Truth in a similar way to which the Ineffable Name of Deity symbolizes, for us, Deity itself (Mackey 1882).

In the 5th Degree the number 9 is used again when Adoniram is ordered by Solomon to prepare a funeral consistent with the virtues of Hiram, and in 9 days he prepared a mausoleum and ordered all the Craft to be present.

In the 6th Degree we find the Lodge illuminated by 3 candlesticks, each having 9 branches and forming 3 equilateral triangles. Here again we have another rendition of the square of 3 depicting numerically in flaming lights the Ineffable Name and also in triangular form which almost always represents Deity. Additionally, there is now reference to a triune nature as well. Also, on the apron flap for this degree we find an equilateral triangle with the Hebrew letters Yod He or Y H on the apron itself.

The 7th Degree demonstrates the first two letters of the Ineffable Name on the apron both in Hebrew and in Phoenecian characters while the numerical composition of the Ineffable Name is composed of the 3 sided triangle, 5 lights illuminating the Lodge, (1 in the East, 2 in the West, 1 in the south, and 1 in the North) and of course, the 7 Judges and Provosts central to the theme of the degree. Hence the necessary 3, 5, and 7 equating to 15 and again transliterating to Yod He.

The 8th Degree is styled Intendant of the Building. Here the Lodge is lighted with 27 candles comprised of three groups of 9 in the East, South, and West. Again the square of three is evident three times over. Moreover, the Blazing Five-Pointed Star hangs in the East and is emblazoned with the Hebrew letters Yod, He, Vauv or the Samaritan letters of the same.

We can make the case again in the 9th Degree based on the 9 virtues necessary in the pursuit of Justice. They include: Disinterestedness, Courtesy, Devotedness, Firmness, Generosity, Self-Denial, Heroism, and Loyalty. Additionally, 9 Craftmen were appointed by King Solomon to pursue the murderers of Hiram.

The 10th Degree depicts the apprehension of the remaining two ruffians through the additional appointment by King Solomon of 6 additional Craftmen. The total number of Craftmen is 15. Furthermore, the Lodge is again lighted with 3 sets of 5 lights. Again, we have 15, which has been shown to transliterate to Yod He.

In the 11th Degree it is said that the age of an Elu of the Twelve is 18 years (Pike 1982), $(2 \times 9 = 18)$. The 9th, 10th, and 11th Degrees are called the elect degrees and in each the Ineffable Name is either evident directly through the sum of 15 or through deriving the numerical value of 15 through the Pythagorean Talisman.

In the 12th Degree a black and white interlaced Seal of Solomon hangs in the East and in the center is the Ineffable Name in Phonecian letters. If the black and white triangles making up the Seal of Solomon are taken to represent the duality of nature, i.e. the male and the female, it is but a mere extension to extrapolate to the Yod He where the Yod is masculine and the He feminine.

In the 13th Degree we are presented with the Cubical Stone in the Royal Arch of Solomon which derives from the Legend of Enoch. On the face of the Cubical Stone is an equilateral triangle containing the Ineffable Name. This is further reinforced by the lines of the cubical stone which are 9 when looking at it face on.

The Cubical Stone is a connecting symbol between the 13th and the 14th Degrees. Wherein the 14th Degree concludes the Lodge of Perfection we find the Ineffable Name presented in the Cubical Stone, in the 9 Arches of the subterranean vault, in the 3, 5, and 7 lights illuminating the South, West, and the Altar of Obligation. We find it displayed in the Lesser Tetractys as the Seal of Solomon depicting the equilibrium of the contraries as in the Yod (masculine) and the He (feminine), and in the 9 visible lines of the cube, and as Hutchens illustrates, in the Phoenician characters on the jewel of this degree.

The Ineffable Name is evident repeatedly throughout the Degrees of Perfection. It is readily found in written characters on aprons, jewels, and symbols. Moreover, we can now identify the Ineffable Name encrypted numerically in each of the Degrees of Perfection. We find the same to be true throughout many of the later degrees as well. In the other bodies we find it in more complex patterns of constellations, Tribes of Israel, triangles upon squares, chains of triangular links, and lengthy transliterations from Phoenician to Greek to Hebrew to numerical values, and they always resolve into the Symbolic Name of Deity in preparation for each of us receiving the Royal Secret and mastering its application.

Bibliography:

1) Book of Exodus, Chapter iii, vs. 15

2) Book of Exodus, Chapter vi, vs. 2-3

3) Hutchens, R., Albert Pike's Lecture on Masonic Symbolism: The Omkara & Other Ineffable Words, Transcribed and annotated by Illustrious Rex R. Hutchens 33°, Grand Cross and Grand Master of Masons in Arizona, The Scottish Rite Research Society, Washington, DC, 2006, pp.180-181

4) Hutchens, R., A Bridge To Light, 2nd Edition, The Supreme Council 33° of the Ancient & Accepted Scottish Rite of Freemasonry, Southern Jurisdiction, USA, 1995, p.95

5) Mackey, A.G., Symbolism of Freemasonry: Illustrating and Explaining Its Science, Philosophy, Its Legends, Myths and Symbols, Clark and Maynard, New York, 1882, pp. 176-197, p. 225

6) Pike, A., Legenda of the Lodge of Perfection, Southern Jurisdiction, USA, 1956, p. 11

7) Pike, A., Liturgy of the Ancient & Accepted Scottish rite of Freemasonry for the Southern Jurisdiction of the United States, Part 1, IV-XIV, Reprinted Goetz Printing Company, Springfield, VA, 1982, pp, 12, 112, 129

8) Webster's New Collegiate Dictionary, G & C Merriam Company, Springfield, MA, 1981, p. 32, footnote 4

Notes & Appendix:

The ritual of the Scottish Rite degrees is based largely on the revisions and organization of Albert Pike who established continuity and consistency to a hodge-podge of ancient, albeit disjointed Masonic degrees. These degrees have been commented upon, explained and illustrated by many others, some of whom are referenced herein. Pike makes frequent use of the Ineffable Name symbolism in the Hebrew, Phoenician and Samaritan scripts in direct written, as well as more indirectly in alpha-numerical, transliteration. Attached here for the reader's reference are examples of the Hebrew, Phoenician, and Samaritan alphabets as well as the language lineage to help demonstrate the variances and similarities between these languages of the early millennia. For clarification purposes the numerical equivalent in the Hebrew from aleph (A) to Yod (Y) are in sequential order 1-10 where Aleph is the number 1, He is number 5 and Yod is number 10.

Major Alphabets

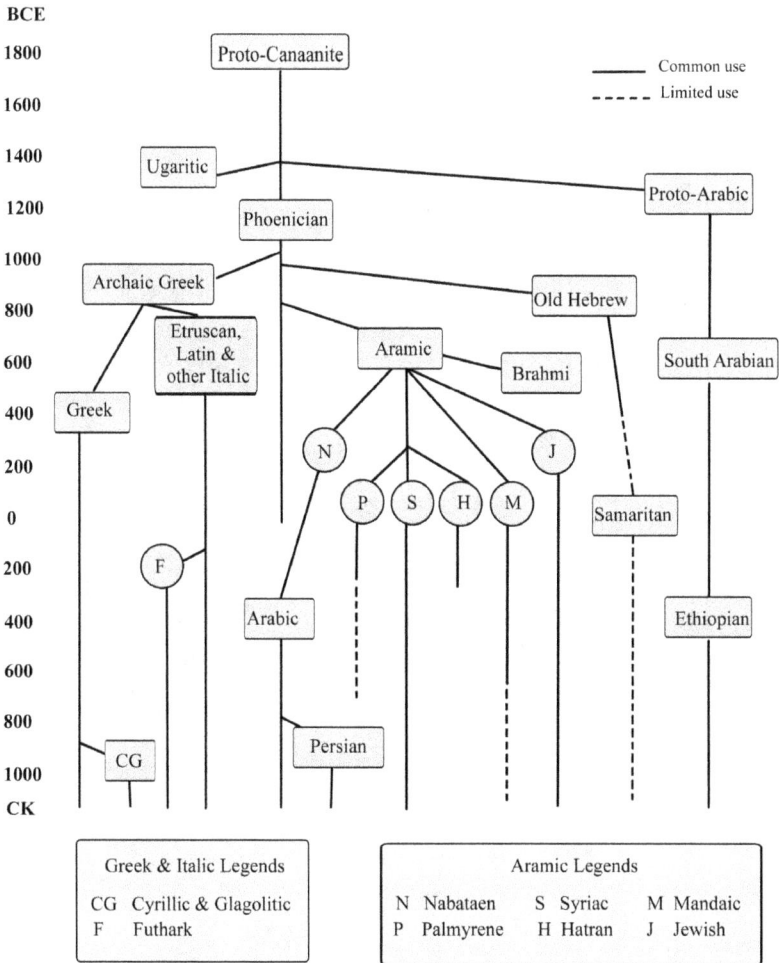

Major Alphabets chart showing the descent of writing systems from Proto-Canaanite (c. 1800 BCE) through Phoenician, Aramaic, Greek, and other branches.

Timeline (BCE to CK):
BCE 1800, 1600, 1400, 1200, 1000, 800, 600, 400, 200, 0, 200, 400, 600, 800, 1000, CK

Legend: —— Common use; - - - - Limited use

Boxes and nodes:
Proto-Canaanite, Ugaritic, Phoenician, Proto-Arabic, Archaic Greek, Old Hebrew, Etruscan, Latin & other Italic, Aramic, Brahmi, South Arabian, Greek, N, J, P, S, H, M, Samaritan, F, Arabic, Ethiopian, CG, Persian

Greek & Italic Legends

CG Cyrillic & Glagolitic
F   Futhark

Aramic Legends

| N | Nabataen | S | Syriac | M | Mandaic |
| P | Palmyrene | H | Hatran | J | Jewish |

From Lawrence Lo 1995-2010; AncientScripts.com

Forms and Pronunciation of Hebrew-Samaritan Scripts

	I	II	III	IV	V	VI	VII	VIII	IX	X	
			Majuscule				Minuscule				
א											ā'lāf
ב											bīt
ג											gā'mān
ד											dā'lāt
ה											īy
ו											bā
ז											zēn
ח											īt
ט											ṭīt
י											yūt
כ											kāf
ל											lā'bāt
מ											mīm
נ											nūn
ס											sin'gāt, sin'kāt
ע											in
פ											fī
צ											ṣā'diy
ק											qūf
ר											rīš
ש											šān
ת											tāf

Description: The evolution of the Samaritan script

Source: http://www.mystae.com/reflections/messiah/scripts/alphabet.html

Date: Unknown

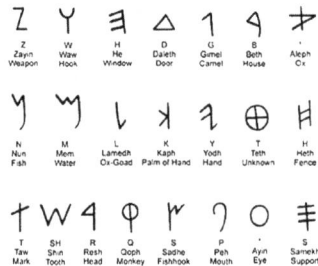

The Phoenician Alphabet ~ 1400 BC

Z — Zayin — Weapon
W — Waw — Hook
H — He — Window
D — Daleth — Door
G — Gimel — Camel
B — Beth — House
Aleph — Ox

N — Nun — Fish
M — Mem — Water
L — Lamedh — Ox-Goad
K — Kaph — Palm of Hand
Y — Yodh — Hand
T — Teth — Unknown
H — Heth — Fence

T — Taw — Mark
SH — Shin — Tooth
R — Resh — Head
Q — Qoph — Monkey
S — Sadhe — Fishhook
P — Peh — Mouth
Ayin — Eye
S — Samekh — Support

TWENTY-FIRST CENTURY PHILOSPHICAL DIFFERENCES

By John L. Palmer

As the editor of a national Masonic magazine, I receive many letters to the editor and articles submitted for publication. In my case, most of them are about Freemasonry, Templary, or Christianity. Of those about Freemasonry, several are from Brethren expressing opinions about the great controversy about where our leadership should be leading us at this time of crisis in our Fraternity.

As I read and try to understand all this dialogue back and forth, questions come to mind. Is there a crisis in our Fraternity? If so, what are our options? What exactly are those who are offering suggestions wanting us to do? Is there agreement on even the definition of the crisis? How did we get to this point? How many different opinions are there? Which side should I take? How can I help?

Let us explore this situation, try to determine what the facts are, use some logic, and see if we can try to sort this thing out so that we can make some informed, intelligent decisions and take action that will benefit the Fraternity. Above all, let us see if we can achieve or re-establish harmony among the Craft. Is there a win-win to be had over all this?

Now you are probably asking, "which crisis, which conflict is he referring to?" Let's define the subject first.

The Neo-Moderns

Sometime around the late 1970's the number of Freemasons in the United States peaked out and began to decline. In the known history of Freemasonry, at least since we have been counting Freemasons, the number of members in our Fraternity has gone up and down, but this was, by far, the largest number of members we had ever had. When I speak of Freemasonry, I include the Blue Lodge of Symbolic Freemasonry and all the other organizations [that] either predicate their membership on the Lodge or are in some way associated with it. I generally refer only to Freemasonry within the United States. The fraternity had established an elaborate and extensive internal infrastructure. Each of our bodies had employees at the state and national level and many at the local level. In addition, most of the bodies had established statewide or national philanthropies [that] employed literally thousands of people. We had hospitals, orphans homes, retirement communities, foundations, and educational institutions. In addition to the payrolls, we had inherited or built huge numbers of buildings.

We had Lodge buildings, Grand Lodge buildings, Scottish Rite Temples, York Rite Temples, Shrine Temples, orphanages, hospitals, museums, libraries, and schools, not to mention the office space necessary to administer all this infrastructure. All these were supported financially by our members through dues, contributions, fund raising efforts, and sometimes return on investments which some of our wiser predecessors had established for that purpose.

As the number of members began to decline, our leadership was faced with an issue that none of their predecessors in their memory had faced. Either shrink the infrastructure costs, or place a burden on the members. You notice that I did not say, "increase the burden on their members" because as the numbers had gone up during the preceding fifty years, the financial demands on each member had decreased in terms of real purchasing power to a point that it was only a small fraction of what it had once been. Inflation and the consumer price index continued to rise each year and the cost of dues remained the same or even decreased in some instances. This situation was exacerbated by the nature of our real estate holdings. During the first half of the 20th Century, the Fraternity had erected elaborate and impressive buildings all over the country and these buildings had generally not been well maintained. They were, in some cases, literally falling down around us and had historical significance not only to the Fraternity, but to the communities in which they were located.

As the financial pressure increased, the first to try to address it were understandably the Scottish Rite of the Southern Jurisdiction, the Shrine, and to a lesser degree, the Grand Lodge of Pennsylvania. Why "understandably?" Because they were very large organizations, centrally managed, and in the case of the Shrine and the Scottish Rite, they had extensive real estate holdings. The hard decisions hit these organizations first. Rightly believing that the source of the problem lay with the Blue Lodge because all their membership was derived from the Lodge, the Scottish Rite and the Shrine decided to try to engage the leadership of the Grand Lodges in formulating a solution to the "problem." They brought the problem and laid it at the feet of the Conference of Grand Masters of North America. This resulted in the formation of a "Masonic Renewal Committee." This committee, realizing that they needed more data to make a good decision, hired consultants to gather the data, analyze it, and make recommendations. From this effort several recommendations were offered. Some acknowledgement was made that our members should be better educated about the fraternity. More popular member activities should be adopted. Our existing members should face the fact that they need to step up to the plate and, as individuals, share a greater amount of the financial responsibility by raising dues or conducting more fund raisers, but far and above, the clearest message from the consultants, and hence from the committee, was that we needed to increase the number of members, or at least decrease the "bleeding" loss of members each year. It was suggested that Freemasonry had fallen behind the times and was not responsive to the needs of the current generation. It was touted that the modern prospect was not interested in ritual and didn't have the time to spend night after night at lodge meetings because of the work and family demands of our modern society. It was even stated that we appeared to be discouraging men from becoming Masons because of our policy of non-solicitation, our demands that initiates memorize and recite back pages of lectures, and the long three to five months required to complete the initiation process. So the recommendations included proposals to reduce or eliminate the need for any memorization, to reduce the time and effort required to become a Mason and even to have one day classes where a man could lay down his money, attend a half day or full day meeting, observe what was going on, and go home at the end of the day as a bona fide, card carrying, Master Mason. In addition, there were recommendations concerning the visibility of the Fraternity. After all, we would need to advertise to attract good prospective Masons. Out of this came the recommendations that our buildings be opened to the public more than ever before, that our charities and their benefits be publicized more than ever, and that our fund raising activities for our charities increase and involve more public participation. In order to attract the right sort of men, it would be necessary that we make them aware of the good things we do.

Now considering the definition of the word "crisis" as a time of significant change, everyone on all sides of this issue seemed to agree that there was a crisis. Many of the Grand Lodges took the recommendations of the committee and began immediately to implement the suggestions. Others rebelled.

The ones who were on board with the recommendations of the committee began to confer one day classes, to allow solicitation, to relax memorization standards, to adopt publicity campaigns. They often touted that the Masonic family of organizations donated over two million dollars each day to charity. Open houses and "bring a friend" nights began to spring up almost everywhere. This was the genesis of the group [that] constitutes one of the factions in the debate about where we should head in the twenty-first century. I shall call them the "neo-moderns" in memory of that faction of Freemasons called the "Moderns" in the eighteenth and early nineteenth century division that occurred in our Fraternity.

At about the same time, or perhaps a little earlier, a Lodge in Australia was dealing with the same, or at least a similar problem of declining membership and interest, and in response to their problem, proposed an entirely different type of solution. They decided that the reason that membership was declining was that their own membership, and therefore the public, really did not understand what Freemasonry really was, that as a result, the Lodge had been changed into something entirely different than it was intended to be, and that the members and prospective members were apathetic about this "new" organization called Freemasonry, not Freemasonry itself. They noted that emphasis had shifted from fellowship, philosophical study, and spiritual development into stale donuts, casual dress, and superficial discussion about mundane topics like how the roof should be repaired. They insisted that if the Fraternity would return to what they believed it once was, men, both members and non-members would be attracted and the problem would solve itself. They insisted that men were attracted to things that they perceived to be valuable and that lodge membership should be portrayed as being of immense value in order to attract men who would profit from the intellectual spiritual growth the Fraternity offers. Putting their theory into practice, they created a Lodge with dues ten to one hundred times higher than the ones they had been paying. They required that members dress formally and to some degree uniformly. They placed emphasis on intellectual discussions of Masonic philosophy and history, and they reduced the number of meetings, thereby eliminating much of the opportunity to scrap over the cost of building insurance or how the roof should be repaired.

Throughout the United States, there were a number of Freemasons who were not really happy with what was going on with their lodges. When they finally obtained membership in the Fraternity they were disillusioned. When they saw what the Freemasons actually did in their meetings, they were greatly disappointed. They had expected stately, impressive ceremonies; profound discussions of subjects which would challenge them mentally, and the opportunity to learn of great mysteries to which they would have otherwise not been privy. Many of these young Freemasons were senior DeMolays. They had great respect for the Fraternity before they petitioned and for the men they knew as Freemasons, but something was missing. They saw instead Masters conferring degrees clad in flip–flops, cutoffs, and a tee shirt advertising beer with holes in it. They were ridiculed if they wore a tie to lodge even though they had seen their grandfathers put on a tie before each lodge meeting. They saw ceremonies which could have been most impressive read from a book by a cast member who read poorly and didn't understand some of the words, much less the meaning of the rituals. They saw men taking solemn obligations to do all sorts of lofty things and then promptly behaving as if they had not done so. When they asked "why?" about parts of the ceremonies or of the rituals, they were told just to memorize the words correctly, that nobody knew why they said what they did. They saw men arguing ceaselessly over whether to spend small amounts of money to fix a toilet in the lodge that these same men would not have hesitated one second to have repaired in their homes. They looked at the shabby, ill maintained and sometimes just dirty buildings, and they asked themselves, "what have I gotten myself into?" Isn't there some better place where I want to spend my time?"

Many of these men fell away from the Fraternity, lost and disillusioned. Some, however, actually took the time to learn the ritual, to read the literature, and to think about what Freemasonry ought to be and decided that it needed to return to the institution that they perceived it once had been. They saw what the small group in Australia had done. They learned that this lodge now had a waiting list to become members, and they perceived that this was the Freemasonry that they had bargained for and, by George, they were going to have it. Out of this has grown a fairly new movement in the United States of establishing "Traditional Observance" Lodges or "European Concept" Lodges. These lodges typically have a higher dues structure, dress more formally, meet less frequently, are more demanding of their members, and discuss more esoteric and philosophical subjects. Some also emphasize excellence in the initiatic experience imparted by well done, impressive ritual. Although there are subtle differences in these types of lodges, they fall under the umbrella of what some call "Masonic Restoration," and there has, indeed, been an organization established to promote these ideals. Of course, many of the members who do not see eye to eye with these folks are horrified and have rebelled and tried to suppress this movement. I shall call these folks "Neo-Antients" in honor of the "Antients" who feuded with the "Moderns" two hundred years ago.

The Status Quos

I had been following the rather public debate between the Neo-Moderns and the Neo-Antients for some time when I realized that there exist at least one and possibly two additional groups that are engaged in this discussion. The third group has been in existence much longer than the other two "upstarts." They probably were formed as a result of the formation of this country and they are being blamed by both of the "Neos" for bringing this crisis to us in the first place. This begs three additional questions. "Who are they?" "What is their position?" "Why do they believe as they do?"

Regardless of its origin (take your pick), at the time of the formation of our country, Speculative Freemasonry was a gentleman's organization. This is not to say that tradesmen and soldiers were not members, but they thought of their membership as very prestigious. With the establishment of our country came one of the first practical applications of the idea that all men are created equal and that perceived differences between those of "royal" blood and those who had served as their servants and serfs for centuries should be minimized, if not eradicated. The great American experiment resulted in a country that not only mimicked many of the internal teachings and practices of Freemasonry, but one that provided opportunity for the Fraternity to flourish free from political, religious, or even popular oppression. Flourish it did! Lodges sprang up everywhere chartered by both Ancients and Moderns. Grand Lodges which traditionally had jurisdiction over entire countries were springing up one, or in some cases, two to the state. Good men who would never have had the opportunity to become Freemasons in the old country were joining the Fraternity by the thousands, and thus begun a period of growth unprecedented to Freemasonry. Although the Fraternity has had its ups and downs over the last two hundred years, through wars, depressions, persecution from several religious denominations, the Morgan Affair, and even an Anti-Masonic political party, it has not only survived, but thrived in the environment our country provided. It grew all out of proportion to growth in other countries until roughly half of all the Freemasons in the world were American Freemasons.

Sometime between the beginning of World War I and the end of World War II something different happened. The title "Freemason" was no longer a coveted appellation. The parades of Templars consisting of literally tens of thousands of Sir Knights ceased to occur. The Fraternity began to fade from the public eye. There were large influxes of members following both World Wars, but those who joined became less and less active. One theory for why this happened has to do with the great influx of members after each war. In my state, the number of Freemasons roughly tripled during a fifteen year period after the second world war. Obviously, this was due in part to the high regard that men had for the institution.

Previously the percentage of members attending meetings was fairly high, although I perceive that this percentage had been gradually decreasing over the prior two hundred years. The benevolence of the lodge was most often done in secret so as not to embarrass the recipient. A widow might wake up one fall morning to discover a cord of wood stacked on her front porch. A man down on his luck with children to feed might discover that someone had anonymously paid off his bill at the general store. The Lodge was a place where men interacted with each other socially, at least men of good repute. The members looked upon each other as trustworthy, of good character, honest, and generous. They were the pillars of the community. In early days, discussions at the lodge included philosophy, morality and character building. Some of the esoteric and spiritual nature of the Order had slipped out of the consciousness of the order some time earlier.

The men attended the meetings, enjoyed the fellowship and lively discussion on any number of topics, broke bread together and generally bonded together as adult men who were in this world together and who could best survive its vicissitudes by sticking together and helping one another.

Suddenly things changed. They really didn't understand why, but men were knocking on their doors literally by the hundreds wanting to join the lodge. Since the vast majority of these applicants were good men and since the Lodge was intended to "take good men and make them better," these Masons set to work to accommodate all these applicants. Making men Masons is no easy task. It requires the memorization of pages and pages of ritual [that] had to be letter perfect lest it be changed from generation to generation and become an "innovation." Hundreds and thousands of catechetical lectures must be taught, as many as three per initiate. Degrees had to be scheduled, as many as three per night three times a week. As the work progressed, the Brethren found less time for the lively discussions that had characterized their meetings in the past. Then because of the time factor, it became more difficult to enjoy meals together at the lodge. Even the benevolence became burdensome and our charity migrated to sending money to great centralized offices far away so the resources could be used more efficiently. As the great influx of members finally wound down after fifteen years of furious activity, more than two thirds of the members had never seen Masons do anything of substance other than contribute to centralized charities, initiate new members, and debate mundane issues associated with the maintenance of the property. The new members had certainly not seen anything else. Many of the old members had died or gotten too old to attend. Of the ones left, those who were not interested in taking part in the initiation by performing ritual or teaching lectures had lost interest and ceased to attend. The member who was perceived as most prestigious was the one who was most capable of conferring degrees and teaching lectures. Ritual was king. All honors, including the positions of leadership requiring quite a different set of skills, were awarded to the ones we now call "ritualists." Surprisingly, this did not mean that the ritual being conferred after the great surge was better than that conferred before it. Standards had actually been lowered because of the great demand for men to confer degrees and levels of performance were accepted that would not have been tolerated in the past. Moreover, it was not required that one actually understand what he was saying to the candidate, but it was extremely important that the word "that" not be substituted when the word "which" was called for. Nor was it necessary that the initiate actually understand the lessons taught or the obligations he assumed, just that he not disclose them to anyone outside the Fraternity. In short, it reminds me of a line from the movie "Jaws" describing the nature of a shark. All the Masons were doing were meeting, eating, and making more Masons.

Now let's not be too quick to blame these men for our present day troubles. Faced with the same challenges, there is little doubt in my mind that even knowing what we do now about the result, we would probably do the same thing that they did. We certainly do not want to blame the men who came in during that period. They were the students. They were being taught what Masonry was by the actions of their elders. Unknown to them, these "elders" were simply struggling to keep up with demand. We do, however, need to try to understand their perspective of the Fraternity before we begin to criticize them for clinging to the status quo. I call these men the "Status Quos."

Perceptions and Positions

In reality, both neo-moderns and neo-Antients are reacting against the practices of the status-quos. They just disagree about how the status quo should be radically changed.

Let's look at the perceptions of each of these groups and how it influences the positions they take. I begin with the status-quos. There are really two sub groups under the status-quos, the "actives" and the "inactives." Although the inactives are not major players in the drama that is unfolding, they will have some influence and cannot be ignored. The inactive has been a member of the Fraternity from fifteen to fifty years, but he pays his dues each year although he rarely attends meetings. He contributed to the charities of the Fraternity when asked and may even show up and help with fund raising activities. He is proud of what the Masons do for charity and is proud to be a part of it. He believes Freemasons are good men and is proud to be associated with them. He is not interested in doing ritual or teaching lectures but has great respect for the ones who do these things well. He thinks his son should become a Mason and is intensely proud if he does. He is not aware that there is a crisis and does not understand that there is even disagreement between the neo-moderns and the neo-Antients. He is very happy with the level of his involvement and sees no reason to change anything. Because he is used to the current dues structure which has been in place for his entire Masonic career and because he is receiving nothing more tangible for his dues than a 2"x3" pasteboard card and perhaps a fifty year pin, he is somewhat resistive to any increase in the annual dues. He does not have a vote in the Grand Lodge session and wouldn't attend if he did. Most importantly, he comprises about eighty percent of our present membership.

The other segment of the status-quos consists of the "actives." As I describe them, remember that they are only the active status-quos. Almost all of the neo-moderns and neo-Antients are active.

These are the folks who have kept our fraternity alive for the last fifty years. They respect above all others the ones who can do the ritual in an accurate and impressive manner, although less than ten percent of them actually do this. They are institutionally oriented and generally don't ask why we do the things like we do. They are proud to be members of a fraternity which included so many presidents, heroes, and other celebrities. They have a firm view of the origin and the history of the order and, although they may disagree with each other about these things, they do not consider them to be important enough to argue about. The important thing is that the bills be paid, the building kept habitable, the charities be funded, and the membership cease to decline. They realize that the inactives are the key to the financial survival of the lodge and fear greatly that raising the dues will effect a mass exodus of inactives, bankrupt the lodge, and spell the end of Freemasonry. They believe that Masonic office is primarily a reward for faithful attendance and hard work and feel that the primary duty of the leadership is to serve the brotherhood by extolling the virtues of Freemasonry, primarily to the brethren. They see the current decline in numbers as temporary and part of the cyclic nature of the Fraternity. They certainly don't want to be involved in anything that might be termed "occult" and probably do not know the word esoteric. They do not believe that the relaxation of any kind of standards will benefit the Fraternity, but rather that by the introduction of bad materials, it will destroy it by changing it into something entirely different than it was intended to be. They see the neo-Antients as "elitists" believing that they are better than anyone else and fear that the study of philosophy will lead the fraternity down the path of heresy and ignore the prohibition of the discussion of religion in the lodge. They see the neo-moderns as attempting to discard the ritual and lower the standards of character required for membership. They see impending disaster but believe it is still possible to convince the inactives to become active and that the neos of both varieties will either go away or just give up and demit. They continue to advise new initiates of the evils of both the neo-Antients and the neo-moderns but with decreasing success. At the same time, remember that, for the most part, these are the men who are actually holding the Fraternity together at this time.

So where do the neo-moderns stand and why? These folks are businessmen. They understand the value of the bottom line and they are men of action. If something is broke, you fix it. The two things that are broken about Freemasonry is that we don't have enough members to support our charities and infrastructure, let alone influence society outside our organization, and that we don't have enough money to pay our bills. They believe that the active status-quos approach to finances of simply cutting the budget each year is undermining the purposes of the fraternity and will ultimately fail. They firmly believe that substantial dues increases to offset the loss of numbers will drive off the golden goose of the inactive status-quos and spell the end of the Fraternity. Their primary objective is to preserve the existence of Freemasonry at all costs. The only option left, therefore, is to increase the number of members back up to the level necessary to sustain our charities and infrastructure. It will probably be necessary to sacrifice some of our elaborate and grand buildings along the way. They are practical men. SO how do we increase the numbers? The neo-moderns believe that there are many good men out there who would make good masons, at least good enough to be acceptable. If we can get these men to join to pay the bills, and enough of them to become active in lodge activities attractive to even more men, we can perpetuate the Fraternity indefinitely. They believe that the Fraternity has always evolved and must evolve as the society in which we live continues to change. They agree with the status-quos that we should continue to relax dress requirements so that men will feel comfortable when they come to lodge. They believe that we must include more family activities because today's good young man is much more interested in spending the limited amount of leisure time he has with his young family than in bonding with other men. Due to the increasingly urban and suburban life styles, our prospective member no longer has time to spend night after night at the lodge and untold hours learning lectures. He will be attracted to the order partially because of its good works, so we should continue these on the current level and increasingly advertise our involvement so the best men will be attracted. He does not agree with the neo-Antients that men attracted and initiated this way would be worthless or even detrimental because, after all, they would be paying dues and supporting the charities, and some would even become interested in the ritual and perpetuate the fraternity. Besides, if we run out of ritualists, we now have the modern capability to video tape the whole thing and show it to hundreds at a time. After all, the modern man now learns from videos, not books, and certainly not from an individual sitting alone, mouth to ear; this is too inefficient and the young men aren't even trained to learn that way any more. They no longer have this kind of patience. Isn't the entire ritual published somewhere on the internet anyway, so what is the harm in videotaping it? This is the position of those whom I call neo-moderns, and although some of these folks have tried this approach and decided that it was not successful, these folks seem to be supplanting the status-quos in positions of leadership in several of our Grand Lodges and some of the appendant bodies, notably the Shrine. The shrine has already relaxed its standards to eliminate the requirement of membership in one of the rites. This position of the Shrine is completely understandable. The organization has only two stated purposes, to support the charities and to fellowship. Moreover, they have been among the hardest hit from the membership decline and the cost of the hospitals is spiraling up.

So where do these new kids on the block, the neo-Antients, stand on all this? First, while they are appreciative of the status-quos for preserving the Fraternity all these years, they feel that we have gone too far in the United States with this "on the level" thing. Good Masons allow a marginally "good man" to become a member in the confident expectation that exposure to the Fraternity will polish his rough edges. This man brings in someone who is marginally "less good" than he with the hope that Freemasonry will "make him better." Eventually you have a situation where we are having Masonic trials to try to get rid of those who are damaging the reputation of the Fraternity and destroying its harmony, men who obviously do not have the character to fulfill their obligations or perhaps the understanding to know what they are. Even worse, we are not having these trials, but are rather tolerating this sort of behavior. Our initiates come into the lodge and are suitably impressed by our solemn obligations only to shortly discover that in spite of all these lofty sounding principles, many of our members are blatantly behaving as if they had never heard them. We are then classed as hypocritical by the quality initiate and written off as the fading remnants of something that was at one time surely a great institution. You see, the young man petitioning our lodges is quite different than he was only ten years ago. He has seen all the movies and searched the internet looking for and finding information about the fraternity. He may even have read some of the books. Although the information he has acquired may be true or false, he has a favorable opinion of the fraternity, because he has solicited membership even though he may not actually know a Freemason. He has great expectations of being received into an institution with an ancient history and many mysteries to reveal that will enhance his reputation and satisfy his intellectual curiosity. He does not expect for this endeavor to be easy or to be cheap. Nothing easy and cheap could be that valuable. He expects to have to study and work for what he receives, and expects it to be worth it. He expects his new brethren to be just like him, only better informed. He wants to be part of a mystical brotherhood that has come down from ages past and which is engaged in great and important undertakings; important not only to him but to civilization as a whole.

He is certainly not expecting some sort of superficial civic club where men pretend to be profound and yet understand and behave no better than anyone else he knows. The neo-Antients want to find and initiate this man. They believe that respect for the institution demands that a Brother attending a Masonic meeting be dressed in the best cloths he possesses if he possibly can. On the other hand, if circumstances really dictate that this is a white shirt and bib overalls, he is welcome among them. These Brethren believe in excellence in ritual just like the status-quos, but they insist on the excellence part and believe that the fellow delivering it ought to know what it means and mean it when he says it. Ignorance of the symbolism, history, and philosophy is tolerated, but apathy towards them is not. They simply prefer not to spend their time attending lodge with those who are not interested in these subjects. Fellowship is important to these neo-Antients but frequently in a more formal setting and involving a higher quality of food and surroundings.

They are willing to pay for these things. Contrary to the opinion of the status-quos, they do not believe that they are better than the other brethren, but they do believe that they should be allowed to form lodges so they can associate primarily with brethren of similar interests. These neo-Antients have very high standards of conduct and for the consideration of prospective Masons. They believe that just because a man appears to be of good character that he is not necessarily "entitled" to membership in their lodge, and that if he is not a good fit concerning his opinions and interests, as a member, he might disrupt the harmony of the lodge. The number of members in these lodges is normally limited because the members desire to cultivate a very close relationship with every other member of the lodge. They believe that this would be difficult to do with a large number of members. On the other hand, these Brethren believe that if you are not interested enough to attend most all the meetings of the lodge, you may have been motivated to join for reasons with which they do not agree. There should not be inactive Masons. Although they agree with the neo-moderns that change is necessary, they differ from them in several significant ways. They believe that the initiatic experience, including the ritual, is extremely important. They believe that men are attracted to institutions such as ours not by the price or by the ease of obtaining membership, but that just the opposite is true. The more difficult it is to obtain a thing, the more valuable it seems. They also believe that the institution should deliver on its promises by providing quality associations and intellectually stimulating information, not to mention good food. These brethren are willing to pay for this experience, often several times what they pay for dues in another status-quo lodge. The approach of the neo-moderns seems to the neo-Antients to be perverting what they perceive as the mission of the fraternity and changing it into something entirely different from what it originally was just in order to preserve the name "Freemasonry," not an organization totally different than the original.

MASONIC TEMPERANCE

By Dr. David E. Stafford

Prelude

Freemasonry is an institution that is closely tied to its traditions. Most lodges have personal traditions that are time honored and thought of as indispensible. These traditions work together with the principles and Landmarks of Freemasonry to make the Craft an institution that is rich and alluring; however, Freemasonry suffers from the problem of forming traditions at an uncontrollable rate. The experiences that any profane has while traveling through his three degrees are the experiences that man feels are the cornerstone traditions of the lodge. Examples of this are easy to point out. Members of individual lodges have had heated debates whether or not to have meals at all three degrees or if meals should be reserved for the Master Masons Degree. Each mason is boisterous that the traditions of the lodge dictate one way or the other because that is how it was when he came through the lodge. The funny thing is, this debate usually has nothing to do with tradition and everything to do with the simple reality of who the Worshipful Master was when a particular mason took his degrees. It could probably even be said that it is decided by the Master's work schedule and whether he can make it to lodge early enough to have a meal! Yet, each mason views his personal experience as the traditions of the lodge. This anecdote may seem a little silly to the reader, but with a careful examination of most any lodge, the reader could find a similar debate to be had. With this said, how does anyone know what really is Masonic Tradition? There is no straight forward answer, but it may be asserted that those things that have been practiced within the lodge historically form its foundation, but those things that are connected to the rituals and culture of the Order itself are clearly Masonic tradition.

Introduction

Freemasons are taught that there are four cardinal virtues. These cardinal virtues form some of the earliest Masonic teaching within any Mason's life. The lessons and examples set forth to a new Mason within the lectures on the virtues are both noble and grand; however, it may be argued that the misinterpretation of one of these virtues has caused a major deviation in Masonic tradition throughout the American Craft. The virtue in question is Temperance. Temperance in recent Masonic history has had a convoluted meaning. It has been used to mean a vast array of things from having control over one's passions to complete and total abstinence of the consumption of alcohol, either in general or at any Masonic events. It is this latter interpretation of the term with which this paper would like to combat.

The following pages will examine the meaning of the word temperance in the English language, the use of the word temperance in the Masonic ritual, the traditions of the lodge in reference to alcohol, the moral aspect of the moderate consumption of alcohol, and how the "temperance movement" changed the view of the meaning of temperance. This paper will conclude with a recommendation for modern Freemasonry based upon the findings of this work.

Defining Temperance

In an etymologic journey to trace the meaning of temperance, perhaps the best place to begin is with the Great Light of Masonry, which is "the rule and guide of our faith and practice". (1) Strong's Hebrew and Greek Dictionaries is an excellent port from which to depart. Within the King James Version (KJV) Bible, the word most readily translated as temperance is εγκράτεια or egkrateia (G1466). It is in a noun form meaning "self control (especially continence):—temperance". (2) Egkrateia is used four times in the Bible, in Acts 24:25, Galatians 5:23, and II Peter 1:6. Each of these verses refer to man tempering or subduing his passions. Thayer's Greek Definitions gives an expanded definition compared to Strong's. Thayer defines egkrateia as "the virtue of one who masters his desires and passions, especially his sensual appetites". (3)

The verb form is εγκρατεύομαι or egkrateuomai (G1467), means "to exercise self-restraint (in diet and chastity): . . . contain, be temperate". (4) Egkrateuomai is referenced twice within the Bible, I Corinthians 7:9 and 9:25. The former is translated as "contain" and the latter as "temperate". εγκρατής or egkratēs is the adjective form of egkrateia and is translated as temperate within the KJV Bible, Titus 1:8. (5) Strong defines it as "strong in a thing (masterful), that is, (figuratively and reflexively) self-controlled (in appetite)". (6)

In Titus 2:2, temperate is translated from a different Greek word. In this case, temperate is derived from σώφρων or sōphrōn (G4998). (7) Strong defines sōphrōn as "safe (sound) in mind, that is, self-controlled (moderate as to opinion or passion):—discreet, sober, temperate". (8) Thayer defines it as "1) of a sound mind, sane, in one's senses 2) curbing one's desires and impulses, self-controlled, temperate". (9) In the examination of these words within the KJV Bible, it is clear that being self-controlled, moderate, and sound in thought is the purpose of the Greek roots for the words translated as temperance.
reek tradition and society. It would therefore be reasonable to examine how the Ancient Greeks viewed temperance.

The Ancient Greeks and Temperance

The New Testament was written in Greek to people who were primarily of Greek tradition and society. It would therefore be reasonable to examine how the Ancient Greeks viewed temperance. The Greek world took great strides in detailing the human characteristics that made a man good. These characteristics they called virtues, and within Greek society is where the four Masonic cardinal virtues were conceived and formed. The Greek word sōphrōn is the base word to sophrosyne. Sophrosyne may not be well known to modern day Americans; however, it was a word of great power and meaning to the Ancient Greeks. It delineated the virtue of temperance. Sophrosyne is a word that is very difficult to translate into English due to the limited breadth of the English language. Modern scholars sum up the meaning of the word by quoting the Delphic Codes, or sayings of the Oracle of Delphi, "know thyself" and "nothing in excess". (10) Euripides (480-406 BCE), the prolific Greek dramatist, defined temperance as self-restraint. Helen North in discussing Euripides and his teachings on temperance expressed that "only now does it (temperance) regularly have such connotations as chastity, sobriety, continence, in preference to the older implications—good sense, soundness of mind, sanity—although these are by no means forgotten." (11)

Within Plato's dialogues, it is revealed that Plato saw Socrates as the epitome of temperance or sophrosyne. In Plato's dialogue Charmides, Socrates and his followers debate the meaning of temperance. Throughout the dialogue, the group of philosophers discuss the handsomeness of a particular young boy, and through their innuendos of sexual pleasure from looking at his naked body, the debate over the meaning of temperance begins. As is typical in Plato's work, a definite clear cut answer is never given. Although the general consensus is that Plato defines temperance (sophrosyne) as sober mindedness and moderation.12 Plato also generally described all of the virtues as opposites of a vice. Temperance, Plato saw as the opposite of profligacy (13), or "a state of being abandoned in moral principle and in vice". (14)

In contrast to Plato's theory of opposite virtues and vices, Aristotle taught that virtues were the mean between two vices. (15) Known as the golden mean, Aristotle's belief on virtues taught that between two vices, one of excess and one of deficiency, lay the desirable and noble characteristics to which all men should strive. Fortitude for example is found between recklessness and cowardice. Temperance is found between overindulgence and insensibility. (16) Once again, the reader is presented with evidence that the true meaning of the term and philosophy of temperance is moderation, and although this is an examination in brief, there is no evidence of temperance ever having a meaning of abstinence within the ancient society.

A Modern Definition

Most Worshipful Brother Benjamin Franklin spoke of temperance and virtues in his autobiography. He complained that too many terms and definitions were applied to all of the individual virtues, so instead of applying so many different meanings to a single virtue, Franklin applied only a simple idea for each. Franklin explains his thoughts using the virtue of temperance, how convenient for the topic at hand.

Temperance, for example, was by some confined to eating and drinking; while by others it was extended to mean the moderating every other pleasure, appetite, inclination, or passion, bodily or mental, even to our avarice, and ambition. I proposed to myself, for the sake of clearness, to use rather more names, with fewer ideas annexed to each, than a few names with more ideas; and I included under thirteen names of virtues, all that at that time occurred to me as necessary or desirable; and annexed to each a short precept, which fully expressed the extent I gave to its meaning. . . . 1. Temperance—Eat not to dullness; drink not to elevation. (17)

Franklin listed temperance above all other virtues because he felt "it tended to procure that coolness and clearness of head, which is so necessary". (18) Anyone with any understanding of Franklin's lifestyle knows that he cannot be used to definitively define the meaning of temperance, but to "drink not to elevation" would lead one to believe that in Franklin's view, temperance in drink meant drinking in moderation and not to drunkenness.

In a 1775 publication, The New Universal Etymological English Dictionary printed for William Cavell in London, temperance is defined thusly:

TEM'PERANCE(temperar.tia, L.) moderation, a restraining of our affections and passions, Temperance is one of the four cardinal virtues, and is by moralists said to constitute honesty, or decency and bashfulness. The two species of it are Sobriety, which moderates our eating and drinking; and Chastity, which sets bounds to the enjoyment of conjugal love. Temperance hath also its potential parts, as meekness, clemency, modesty.

TEMPERANCE (with Divines) is defined to be a virtue that consists in an abstinence from sensual pleasures, which renders the body tame and governable, and so serviceable to the soul, and also cheerful in the exercise of religion; which sets the mind of man free from the captivity of sense, and establishes its dominion over, the brutish part, so that the man lives by faith, and not by sense, and is disengaged from the world, and the allurements of it. (19)

It is admitted that the term abstinence is seen within the definition given for temperance in relation to the religious world; however, it should also be admitted that the term is used in reference to all worldly and sensual pleasures. The given definition would refer to abstinence to sex, gourmet foods, alcohol, and any source of worldly or carnal pleasure. It can hardly be argued by anyone that temperance literally means the total abstinence of all fleshly pleasure, at least not anyone who has enjoyed the fruits of such pleasure at least once in his life.

To move the examination of the term temperance specifically to the American colonies and narrowed in reference to the topic of alcohol, it will be prudent to begin with the first true comprehensive American dictionary, Noah Webster's American Dictionary of the English Language, 1828 version. (20) Another reason for beginning the study with the 1828 dictionary is that it predates the overbearing influence of the temperance movement, or the movement to promote the total abstinence of the consumption of alcohol, that had such a dramatic influence upon American society. (21)

This historic work is considered to be both authoritative and conservative. (22) It defines temperance thusly:

TEM'PERANCE, n. [L. temperantia, from tempero.] 1. Moderation; particularly, habitual moderation in regard to the indulgence of the natural appetites and passions; restrained or moderate indulgence; as temperance in eating and drinking; temperance in the indulgence of joy or mirth. Temperance in eating and drinking is opposed to gluttony and drunkenness, and in other indulgences, to excess. 2. Patience; calmness; sedateness; moderation of passion.

Attention should be directed to the fact that total abstinence is nowhere to be discerned from this definition. Temperance, per Webster, is clearly moderation only. Moderation in drink (alcohol) according to this definition would be the occasional intake of alcohol or the moderate intake of alcohol on a more regular basis. The definition of temperance continued to be the same through the 1857 version of An American Dictionary of the English Language, published by J.B. Lippincott; however, by 1896 in G. and C. Merriam's Webster's Collegiate Dictionary, the definition of temperance had been expanded to include abstinence. The definition follows:

Tem'per ance (-ans), n. 1. Habitual moderation in the indulgence of the appetites and passions; specif., moderation, and sometimes abstinence, in respect to using intoxicating liquors. 2. Patience; calmness. 3. Temperature. (23)

By the time the New Websterian 1912 Dictionary: Based upon the unabridged dictionary of Noah Webster was published by Syndicate Publishing Company, the definition of temperance had evolved to be: "moderation, especially in respect to appetites or passions; patience; sobriety; total abstinence". (24) The current definition on the Merriam-Webster online dictionary is:

1: moderation in action, thought, or feeling: restraint; 2a: habitual moderation in the indulgence of the appetites or passions b: moderation in or abstinence from the use of alcoholic beverages. (25)

This simple and quick survey of dictionaries from 1828 through today, which is not meant to be comprehensive by any means, seems to reveal a swinging of a pendulum. In 1828 through at least 1857, the definition of temperance strongly supports the conclusion that temperance means moderation in all things. In 1896, we see temperance being suggested to sometimes mean "abstinence, in respect to using intoxicating liquors", and by 1912, the definition's pendulum moved in the direction of total abstinence being a consistent optional meaning for temperance. As we look at the current definition, we see that the pendulum seems to have readjusted with the use of terminology like "moderation in or abstinence from the use of alcoholic beverages". (26) What can account for this change in the American use of the word? In order to fully answer this question, another voyage through history will have to be taken. Only this time, the focus of the excursion will be directly related to the history of alcohol.

The History of Alcohol

Alcohol has been with man for thousands of years, and its history is as rich and full as the finest glass of Cabernet Sauvignon. As far back in antiquity as 3000 BCE, clay tablets document the use of beer for "sacramental and religious rituals" in Mesopotamia. (27) Archeological evidence supports the assertion that beer and fermented beverages were used daily as far back 10000 BCE. (28) Wine, in a cultured sense, dates as far back as 4000 BCE in Egypt and at least 2500 BCE in Mesopotamia. (29)

It is often forgotten that the Egyptian god Osiris was not only the god of death but was also hailed as the lord of wine. (30) Wine in Ancient Egypt was expensive and was associated with the wealthy, and it was often placed in tombs as an offering to the dead. Osiris is also connected to wine through his presiding over vegetation, and he is credited with the introduction of vines to the ancient Egyptians. A third connection between wine and Osiris is the natural habit of grape vines. During the winter months, grape vines die back and wither into the earth only to be revived and become green and fruitful again in spring. (31) Osiris was also occasionally accredited for introducing beer to the ancient peoples. (32)

Whereas wine was expensive and often reserved as a symbol of status and wealth, beer was the drink of the common Egyptian. Beer was brewed in the home as a source of nutrition and refreshment, and the Egyptians, being quite industrious in all things, brewed more than seventeen varieties of beer and twenty-four of wine.

The Babylonians also consumed beer. Their use of alcohol dates back at least to 2700 BC. (33) The Chinese consumed alcoholic beverages since prehistoric times, and they viewed it as a spiritual and mental food rather than one for the physical body. "In ancient times people always drank when holding a memorial ceremony, offering sacrifices to gods or their ancestors, pledging resolutions before going into battle, celebrating victory, before feuding and official executions, for taking an oath of allegiance, while attending the ceremonies of birth, marriage, reunion, departures, death, and festival banquets" (34) Alcohol was always a part of celebrating important events to the Chinese people.

The Greeks were later introduced to alcohol, around 2000 BC. The first drink of popularity was mead. Wine quickly surpassed mead in popularity and daily use as a beverage, for ritual recognitions, for hospitality, and for medicinal purposes. "Contemporary writers observed that the Greeks were among the most temperate of ancient peoples. This appears to result from their rules stressing moderate drinking, their praise of temperance, their practice of diluting wine with water, and their avoidance of excess in general." (35) Even with a culture of temperance, there is evidence that the Greek symposium was often a locale of excess. The symposium focused on intellectual conversations; however, its association may not have always been temperate. "Scholars have traditionally defined the symposium as a nocturnal gathering of aristocratic men who reclined together—usually on dining couches (klinai), to drink wine while enjoying music, poetry, conversation, and various erotic pursuits with both male and female partners" (36) The Greek philosophers generally identified the benefits of moderate wine drinking; however, they warned of the dangers of excess.

The Hebrews mostly likely first became exposed to wine during their Egyptian captivity. The Hebrews were slow to acclimate to the consumption of alcohol into their culture, and it was condemned by the Nazarites and Rechabites. Its use did develop into routine among the Hebrew people though. Wine was soon introduced into the Jewish religious ceremonies and daily life.

There are numerous references within the New Testament that refer to Jesus' use of alcohol. In the seventh chapter of Luke, there is a dialogue concerning attempts to find fault in the character of Jesus and John the Baptist. In reference to John the Baptist, those who opposed him complained that John came neither eating bread nor drinking wine and called John the devil. In comparison, according to Luke, Jesus came eating and drinking and the same men called him gluttonous and a winebibber. Another reference to wine and Christ is found in second chapter of John. At the wedding in Cana, Jesus turned the water into wine, and the wine was of such superior quality that the Governor complimented the bridegroom. It is not being asserted that Jesus accepted the over use of alcoholic beverages, but to state that Jesus was opposed to the entire use of alcohol is not supported in the scriptures. The Apostle Paul wrote in Ephesians 5:18, "And be not drunk with wine, wherein is excess; but be filled with the Spirit". This quote supports the conclusion that drunkenness or excess in wine was not accepted by the early Christians, but a moderate use of alcohol was not prohibited. As afore stated, the monastic culture of the middle ages was the hotbed of new innovations in brewing beer, fermenting wine, and distilling liquors. All of this done under the graces of the church.

During the Middle Ages, alcohol became a source of nourishment, refreshment, and escape from the harshness of reality. The drinks of choice during the period were predominately mead, beer, and fruit wines. The artful crafting of wine making and brewing was preserved in the monastic lives of priests during the dark ages, and the best beers and wines came from monasteries. Monks produced and sold alcoholic beverages in order to finance the spread of their individual order's principal beliefs and way of life. Towns during the Middle Ages began crafting artisan beers that were a source of great pride and identity to towns folk. (37) Perhaps the greatest contribution of the Middle Ages to alcohol was the discovery of the distillation process. The production and use of distilled spirits grew slowly among alchemists, physicians, and monks. (38) The average consumption of alcohol was nearly double per individual what it is today.

The modern period of history marked a move from an agrarian society to one based on industry. While beer and alcohol were still a standard in human society, there began to be a need for less consumption of it. A primary reason for this was the need for an alert workforce. Beer and wine was no longer the preferred drink during the noon meal. Coffee and tea were more productive for the laboring class of an industrialized age. (39) The industrialization in the modern Western world vilified alcohol. Industrialization of an area brings overcrowded housing conditions, immigration, urbanization, crime, poverty, abuse of a working class, and failing health conditions. (40) Humans, being the creatures they are, needed a whipping boy for the ill social effects of urbanization, and the negative effects of urbanization and industrialization were largely blamed on the consumption of alcohol. (41)

By the late 19th century, the movement to limit or abolish the use of alcoholic beverages began to come into a world scene. "Groups that began by promoting temperance - the moderate use of alcohol - would ultimately become abolitionist and press for the complete and total prohibition of the production and distribution of beverage alcohol. Unfortunately, this would not eliminate social problems but would compound the situation by creating additional problems." (42) The additional problems alluded to by Hanson all revolve around the illegalizing of alcohol as a beverage, bootlegging, smuggling, organized crime, and corrupt officials linked to all of the above.

Temperance in Freemasonry

The Entered Apprentice Degree directly speaks of temperance in its dealings with the Four Cardinal Virtues, temperance, fortitude, prudence, and justice. Within this degree, the following is usually found:

TEMPERANCE is that due restraint upon our affections and passions which renders the body tame and governable, and frees the mind from allurements of vice. This virtue should be the constant practice of every Mason; as he is thereby taught to avoid excess, or contracting any licentious or vicious habit, the indulgence of which might lead him to disclose some of those valuable secrets, which he has promised to conceal and never reveal, and which would consequently subject him to contempt and detestation of all good Masons. (43)

This exact verbiage may be seen in the present Tennessee Craftsman as well as the 1883, Fourth Edition of The Masonic Text-Book of Tennessee (44), as well as Duncan's Ritual of Freemasonry. (45) In fact, it is the common language used throughout much of the United States. It is clear this definition used within the ritual of Masonry in no way, either directly or in inference, suggests an interpretation of temperance as total abstinence. There began to be a discrepancy between Masonic ritual and Masonic code in many states following the temperance movement and prohibition. Grand Lodges began to implement provisions within their Masonic codes prohibiting Masons from being involved in the production, sale, or even consumption of alcoholic beverages. For many years in Tennessee, Masons were forbidden from working at a place of business that sold alcohol nor owning interest in a business that distributed alcohol. Most, if not all, Grand Lodges have weakened this extreme prohibitionist era view of alcohol.

The current Masonic Code of the Grand Lodge of Tennessee has dropped the banning of Masons from working in liquor stores and having financial interest in businesses that distribute or sell alcohol. The code does still ban the use of alcohol in any connection to a Masonic meeting, with the exception of ceremonial wine.

4.1116. Alcoholic beverages may not be served in any Lodge hall or Masonic temple, or in connection with any Masonic gathering, or in a building controlled by a Lodge or in which a Lodge has an interest. This is not intended to prohibit the use of ceremonial wine in Masonic or Masonic related ceremonies. As the jurisdiction of the Grand Lodge extends to all individual Masons, each Mason is charged to observe the provisions of this section at all official meetings or gathering convened by any Masonic or other orders or organizations which predicates their membership on Masonic membership or other connection therewith. (46)

This hold over from prohibition is not overly rare. There are still several states, mostly southern, which retain this prohibition. The true irony of this clause deals with the history of the Grand Lodge of Tennessee. Tennessee Lodge #2 was formed under the authority of the Grand Lodge of North Carolina. This lodge met at Love's Tavern on Front Street in Knoxville. The practice of lodges meeting in taverns was extremely common and the norm47. Following lodge meetings, the brethren would have festive boards, or formal dinners, in which entered apprentices served the food and wine to the brethren. This practice today could be interpreted to be in contradiction to Tennessee Masonic Code.

Conclusion

These travels through etymology and history provide the reader with a little better understanding of the meaning of the Masonic Virtue of temperance. It is not the purpose of the intent of the author to influence the current political status of any Masonic Code through this writing, but it is intended help studying Masons to have a better understanding of the virtue of temperance by examining it through historical eyes and not through current cultural eyes, with all of its bias.

Works Cited:

1) *Tennessee Craftsman or Masonic Textbook (2000), p. 10.*

2) *Strong's Hebrew and Greek Dictionaries, G1466.*

3) *Thayer's Greek Definitions, G1467.*

4) *Strong's Hebrew and Greek Dictionaries, G1467.*

5) *Strong's Hebrew and Greek Dictionaries.*

6) *Strong's Hebrew and Greek Dictionaries.*

7) *Strong's Hebrew and Greek Dictionaries, G4998.*

8) *Strong's Hebrew and Greek Dictionaries, G4998.*

9) *Thayer's Greek Definitions.*

10) *James H. Toner, "Temperance and the Profession of Arms" (Air War College, December 1998, http://isme.tamu.edu/JSCOPE99/Toner99. html). Benjamin Jowett, The Dialogues of Plato (eText, http://www.ucm. es/info/diciex/gente/agf/plato/The_Dialogues_of_Plato_v0.1.pdf) 75-78. . W. and R. Chambers, Popular Educator: A Complete Encyclopedia (Cassell, Petter, and Galpin, 1874) 398.*

11) *Helen F. North, "Temperance," in Vol. IV of the Dictionary of the History of Ideas, ed. by Phillip O. Wiener (New York: Scribner, 1973), p.367.*

12) *Benjamin Jowett, The Dialogues of Plato (eText, http://www.ucm.es/ info/diciex/gente/agf/plato/The_Dialogues_of_Plato_v0.1.pdf)75-78.*

13) *Terence Irwin, Plato's Ethics (New York: Oxford University Press, 1995), 90, 153, & 163. Philosophy: A Text with Readings (Boston, MA: Cengage Learning, 2010), 121. George Anagnostopoulos, A Companion to Aristotle(Wiley-Blackwell, 2009), 456-460.*

14) *Noah Webster, A Dictionary of the English Language (New York: Noah Webster, 1828) no page number.*

15) *George Anagnostopoulos, A Companion to Aristotle (Wiley-Blackwell, 2009), 456-460. Sir David Ross & John Lloyd Ackrill, Aristotle (New York: Psychology Press, 2004), 215.*

16) M. Timur, *The Theory of Morals* (Philosophical Library, 1965), 383.

17) Benjamin Franklin, *Autobiography* (Philadelphia: Henry Altemus, 1895), 149.

18) Franklin, 150.

19) No page number.

20) *Webster's American Dictionary of the English Language* was not the first dictionary published in the New World. Webster himself had published his *Compendious Dictionary* earlier; however, Webster's 1828 dictionary was the most comprehensive, with 70,000 entries, version published in the American version of the English language. Thomas Edie Hill, *Hill's Album of Biography and Art* (Danks, 1891), 287. Harry Redcay Warfel, *Noah Webster: Schoolmaster to America* (New York: The McMillian Company, 1936), 345-370.

21) The rise of the Temperance Movement can be traced to the wave of religious revival that began the winter of 1830 and continued throughout 1831, with Charles G. Finney becoming a prominent evangelist. This evangelistic
45movement quickly transformed from being solely a religious movement to being a reform movement. Robert A. Divine, et al, *The American Story* (USA, Addison-Wesley Educational Publishers Inc., 2002) 344-352.

22) *Webster's American Dictionary of the English Language*, 1828, is today revered by Christian conservative as a fundamental tool in studying the Bible. Webster's dictionary includes a mass of biblical references and an attempt to conform to biblical interpretations of the history of language; thusly, it is concluded that the work is conservative in nature.

23) *Webster's Collegiate Dictionary* (Springfield, Massachusetts: G. and C. Merriam, 1896), 837.

24) Page 827.

25) http://www.merriam-webster.com/dictionary/temperance

26) Emphasis added.

27) Maria Gifford, *Alcoholism* (ABC-CLIO, 2009) 2.

28) "However the discovery of late Stone Age beer jugs has established the fact that intentionally fermented beverages existed at least as early as Neolithic period (cir. 10,000 B.C.) . . . and it has been suggested that beer preceded bread as a staple." David J. Hanson, Preventing Alcohol Abuse: Alcohol, Culture, and Control (Westport, CT: Praeger Publishers, 1995) 1.

29) Patrick E. McGovern, The Origins of Wine (Pschology Press, 1996) vi, 112, & 124.

30) John G. Griffiths, The Origins of Osiris and His Cult (Netherlands: E.J. Brill, 1980), 163. Iain Gately, Drink: A Cultural History of Alcohol (New York: Gotham Books, 2009). "The annual rise of the Nile was also associated with Osiris, god of the dead and of life, of vegetable regeneration, and of wine. In the dynastic era, Egypt had become a producer as well as importer of irp. It remained an elite beverage, hence its protection by the most important deity in the Egyptian pantheon."

31) Patrick E. McGovern, Ancient Wine: The Search for the Origins of Viniculture (USA: Princeton University Press, 2003) 135.

32) David J. Hanson, Preventing Alcohol Abuse, Culture and Control (Wesport, CT: Prageger, 1995) 2.

33) David J. Hanson, Preventing Alcohol Abuse, Culture and Control (Wesport, CT: Prageger, 1995).

34) Zhang Pei-Peng, Drinking in China (The Drinking and Drug Practice Surveyor, No. 18) 13.

35) David J. Hanson, Preventing Alcohol Abuse, Culture and Control (Wesport, CT: Prageger, 1995) 3.

36) Michael Gagarin, ed., The Oxford Encyclopedia of Ancient Greece and Rome, Volume 1 (Oxford University Press, 2010) 409.

37) Thomas S. Austin, Alcohol in Western Society from Antiquity to 1800 (Santa Barbara, CA: ABC, 1985).

38) David J. Hanson, Preventing Alcohol Abuse, Culture and Control (Wesport, CT: Prageger, 1995).

39) Thomas S. Austin, Alcohol in Western Society from Antiquity to 1800 (Santa Barbara, CA: ABC, 1985). Jean-Charles Sourina, A History of alcoholism (Oxford: Oxford Press, 1990).

40) Roxanne Friedenfels, Social Change: An Anthology (New York: General Hall, 1998) 229.

41) *Jean-Charles Sourina, A History of Alcoholism (Oxford: Oxford Press, 1990) 20.*

42) *David J. Hanson, Preventing Alcohol Abuse, Culture and Control (Wesport, CT: Prageger, 1995) 11.*

43) *Board of Custodians, Grand Lodge of Tennessee Tennessee Craftsman or Masonic Textbook (Twenty-fourth Edition, January 2000) 33.*

44) *Page 48.*

45) *Malcomb C. Duncan, Duncan'sMasonic Ritual and Monitor (Sweetwater Press, 2007) 60.*

46) *Jurisprudence Committee, The Masonic Code Being a Complete Digest of All the Regulations, Laws, Approved Rulings, Decisions, and Enactments of the Grand Lodge of Tennessee (16th Edition) 4-18.*

47) *Brief History of Tennessee Grand Lodge prepared by the Masonic Education Committee, Grand Lodge of Tennessee.*

AN EXAMINATION OF RESPONSES TO A DECLINE IN SOCIAL CAPITAL, CIVIC ENGAGEMENT AND MEMBERSHIP WITHIN AMERICAN FREEMASONRY

By James M. Kinslow

(Editor's Note the complete Thesis document may be viewed at the Members' Area of our website, http://www.tnlor.org.)

INTRODUCTION

Civic engagement is considered vital for the existence and perpetuation of democracy, especially within America (Coleman 1988; Putnam 2000; Boggs 2002; Fried 2002; Schultz 2002; Lichterman 2006). The study of civic engagement and social capital has influenced the work of many academicians and led to the formation of entire university centers. Furthermore, research and theories concerning civic engagement and social capital have been central in influencing American, European, and global socio-political and economic policy (Putnam 2000; Schultz 2002).

In a general sense, civic engagement can be defined as all collective interaction above the level of the family and below the government (Tocqueville 1838; Coleman 1988; Putnam 2000). The term civic engagement has also been referred to in previous studies as civic interaction, civic participation, and political participation. For the sake of consistency, I use the term civic engagement throughout. In this analysis civic engagement refers to the volunteer based interaction found in religion, interest groups, and membership associations.

Social capital is a term closely associated with the concept of civic engagement (Coleman 1988; Putnam 2000; Fried 2002). Putnam (2000) views social capital as the communal value that arises from social networks; social networks lead people to help one another and the collective good. In other words, social capital and civic engagement are entwined. Social capital is the 'capital' or social 'surplus' that is produced by civic engagement (Coleman 1988; Putnam 2000; Fried 2002). Social capital theory, specifically that of Tocqueville (1838) and Putnam (2000), exhaustively examines the concept of civic engagement.

This research is an exploratory analysis of civic engagement in America. I analyze civic engagement in America by examining Masons in America as a unique example of a volunteer membership association within the framework of social capital theory and civic engagement. different Masonic lodges within Colorado to examine variations in civic engagement.

LITERATURE REVIEW

In this literature review, I first explain key historical and current aspects of social capital theory and how they relate to civic engagement. Next, I demonstrate how the Masons are unique in relation to the theory of social capital. Then, I review specific studies that have examined the Masons with reference to components of social capital theory.

Social Capital Theory Roots: Tocqueville

Tocqueville (1838) never used the term "social capital," yet his primary work, Democracy in America, is considered a foundational work for social capital theory and the study of civic engagement (Coleman 1988; Putnam 2000; Fried 2002; Lichterman 2006). Tocqueville (1838) referred often to the notion of civil society. By civil society, he was referring to all social groups and subsequent actions above the family and beneath the government (Tocqueville 1838; Putnam 2000). Hence, his ideas have had a tremendous impact on contemporary studies of civic engagement, which, by definition, occurs within civil society.

Tocqueville studied American democracy on behalf of the French government during the 1830s. The enlightenment motto of Liberty, Equality, and Fraternity was prominent in the minds of French Aristocrats such as Tocqueville, who were not sure of their future place in the country. In his (1838) observation of American democracy he noted what he thought to be a conflicting relationship between the concepts of freedom and equality, or "equality of conditions" as he deemed it (Putnam 2000; Boggs 2002; Fried 2002). Tocqueville (1838) viewed Americans as over emphasizing the democratic attribute of equality (Putnam 2000; Fried 2002; Lichterman 2006). In his opinion this threatened individual and collective freedom. According to Tocqueville, atomistic individualism is the resulting destructive force developing from equality of conditions. This force is destructive to democratic societies, namely America, because it fosters a soft despotism or tyranny of the majority (Putnam 2000; Fried 2002). That is, the people were fine with relinquishing their freedom so long as they felt equal with others and could elect their own representatives that would ensure that the equality of conditions stayed unimpaired. This prohibited freedom to anyone seeking to rise above the equality of conditions, fostered an individualistic mindset of civic irresponsibility, and led to government by the subtle tyranny of majority decree. Tocqueville (1838) concluded that the solution for this inherent flaw of American democracy was a robust civil society (Putnam 2000; Fried 2002; Lichterman 2006).

Tocqueville (1838) saw civic engagement as the balancing factor between the opposing forces of liberty and equality in America. Civic engagement allowed for the formation of civic groups or entities such as, religion, town hall meetings, and the press (Putnam 2000; Fried 2002).

These civic entities comprised what Tocqueville called "civil society." He viewed civil society as essential for liberty to exist in American democracy and civic activity as not only a right but a responsibility of the individual. He stated: "The Americans have combated by free institutions the tendency of equality to keep men asunder, and they have subdued it" (Tocqueville 1838:195). Thus, free institutions combat (through civic engagement) equality of conditions as viewed by Tocqueville by bringing people together who would have normally remained apart. Tocqueville's ideas have influenced many contemporary theorists. Of special interest in this regard is Robert Putnam, to whom I now turn.

Contemporary Social Capital Theory: Putnam

There are multiple conceptions of social capital. Pierre Bourdieu, Nan Lin, David Schultz, and James Coleman are a few among noted contemporary sociologists who have explored and expounded on the theory of social capital. Robert Putnam is perhaps the most cited and well known social capital theorist. For the purpose of this paper I will analyze the concept of social capital according to the theory of Robert Putnam, who is considered the "modern Tocqueville". While potentially useful for understanding the Masons as a formal organization, formal organizational theories are not covered in this thesis as the focus is not on formal organizations per se but rather on civic engagement and social capital as a result of organizational participation.

Putnam (2000: 19) describes social capital as "connections among individuals - social networks and the norms of reciprocity and trustworthiness that arise from them." Social capital is thus the coordination of group level activity (civic engagement) and the resulting positive societal outcomes. Putnam views civic engagement as positive for the individual and American society (Putnam 2000; Boggs 2002; Fried 2002; Schultz 2002).

Putnam categorizes social capital into two types: bridging and bonding (Putnam 2000; Fried 2002; Schultz 2002). Bridging capital results from "bridging" relationships between existing groups. According to Schultz (2002), bridging capital is similarly individual, such as having access to information that one can use to find jobs. Bonding capital is an increase in capital within a single group. Hence, social capital, according to Putnam, is a positive social force for both the individual and society resulting from civic engagement between (bridging) and within (bonding) social groups.

In Bowling Alone, perhaps Putnam's (2000) most famous work regarding social capital, he presents a massive empirical study which demonstrates a sharp decline in American civic engagement and a corresponding rise in atomistic individualism during the 20th Century, specifically during its latter half (Putnam 2000).

He used several sources of data to document this trend, including data from the Distributive Database Needham Lifestyle archives and from surveys he conducted regarding civic involvement. He analyzed the patterns of membership from 32 charter based civic organizations such as churches and the Girl Scouts and other forms of civic engagement such as voter turnout in Presidential elections (Putnam 2000; Boggs 2002; Fried 2002).

Putnam's conclusion regarding a decline in civic engagement is thus an important negative finding. This research aims to explore the degree to which this apparent decline has affected American civic engagement by examining a prominent voluntary association with a strong and deliberate commitment to civic engagement, namely the Masons.

The Masons

The Masons have existed in America since prerevolutionary times (GLoV 2011; Hollingsworth 2011). They were on the forefront of promoting civic engagement and social capital within a democratic style of government in Europe prior to Colonial America. The Masons teach their members to be civically minded and active, stressing the practice of democratic concepts such as liberty, equality, and civic engagement (GLoV 2011; UGLE 2011). Masons have a democratic style of governance which they were practicing within Masonic Lodges before and during the establishment of those same methods in American government (GLoV 2011; Hollingsworth 2011; UGLE 2011). Hence, the Masons are considered by many to be a prominent organization devoted to civic engagement that has existed from the time of Tocqueville through that of Putnam.

Early American history is filled with activity involving Masons. Numerous members of the American Revolutionary army were Masons. President George Washington was a Mason, along with 17 34 of his generals (The George Washington Masonic Memorial 2011; St. John's Lodge No.1 2011). The majority of the commanders of the continental army were Masons and members of the "Army Lodge." George Washington was sworn in to the presidency by Robert Livingston, also a Mason. The Boston Tea Party was planned at a Masonic Tavern and implemented by Masons. As many as 15 signers of the Constitution were Masons, and 13 signers of the Declaration of Independence. The laying of the Cornerstone for the U.S. Capital Building was a Masonic ceremony (GLoV 2011).

It is thought by many scholars that the Masons have been instrumental in promoting ideas and concepts of social capital and civic engagement throughout the history of America. Since the signing of the Declaration of Independence until the present, approximately 33% of the 112 Supreme Court justices have been Masons. (Hollingsworth 2011; Bessel 2012a) It is commonly assumed that there is a connection between the Masonic affiliation of these men and their participation in creating democracy and social capital in America.

Some may argue that the Masonic Fraternity is anti-democratic, particularly with regard to the treatment of women and minorities. The majorities of Masonic Lodges are male only, and seemingly exclude females from membership. However, Masonic Bodies and Societies do exist for women. The Eastern Star, Job's Daughters, and the Rainbow Girls are but a few Masonic female organizations (GLoV 2012). Further, some Masons claim that due to the nature of the rituals performed, it is better to separate Masonic bodies on the basis of gender. Historically, Masonic Lodges have largely been segregated on the basis of race, specifically between black and white Lodges. Current trends, however, show an increase in racial integration among Lodges (Bessel 2012b). Further, Freemasonry publicly espouses a belief in the equality of mankind without distinction and Masonic membership reflects virtually every race. Prominent non-white Masons include W.E.B. Dubois, Jesse Jackson, Thurgood Marshall, Sugar Ray Robinson, and W.C. Handy.

Many fraternal and civic organizations developed from the Masons. Numerous American Indian, African American, Christian, and women's civic organizations are direct offspring of the Masons (Moffrey 2001; Kaufman and Weintraub 2004). Groups such as The Boy Scouts, The Independent Order of Odd Fellows, The Grange, and The Knights of Pyrthias were all formed by Masons or are offshoots of the Masons (Moffrey 2001; Kaufman and Weintraub 2004; The Independent Order of Odd Fellows 2009). Thus, the Masons are unique to the study of civic engagement in America because they are indirectly responsible for the development of social capital through their involvement in the development of so many civic organizations in America.

Despite their historic influence in developing American democracy and their promotion of civic engagement, the Masons have not been exempt from societal decline in social capital and civic engagement (Putnam 2000). Masonic Lodges began to experience membership declines in the 1960s. This decline has remained consistent year after year up through the present. The Masons have attempted to combat the recent decline in membership in many ways. Chief among their efforts has been the development of two different types of lodges with two very different mechanisms aimed at increasing membership and civic engagement. On the one hand, contemporary lodges (CL) have tried to recruit members by reducing requirements. On the other hand, traditional observance lodges (TOL) have focused on maintaining traditional practices with the hope that this will attract more civically minded recruits.

Traditional Observance Lodges (TOLs) have recently begun to emerge in America (LVX Lodge No. 848 2009; MRF 2010). A TOL is a lodge that promotes a return to a higher standard of membership selection, requirements for progression, and Masonic education for its members (MRF 2010). The argument for TOLs by Masons is that CLs' response to decline in Masonic membership was not merited or beneficial for the organization. TOLs and their supporters argue that a focus on quantity of membership has been at the expense of quality of membership and membership experience. TOLs typically require that a potential member be vetted much more thoroughly than in a CL (MRF 2010; East Denver Lodge No. 160 2011). Lodge membership is capped at TOLs with a typical membership ceiling of around 70 members. TOLs typically require a member to wait at least six months before progressing to the next degree of membership. Members are required to attend a certain number of meetings before progressing. Masonic research papers are often required to be compiled and presented by Masonic candidates and progressing members. Dues and fees are often higher for TOLs compared to their contemporary lodge counterparts (MRF 2010).

Hence, a dichotomy has emerged within the Masons in response to their decline in membership. In CLs there is a focus on raising membership numbers via lowering requirements. The TOLs represent a reaction against the development of CLs, stressing a renewed focus on higher standards for membership. This quantity versus quality dichotomy has possible implications for social capital and civic engagement among the Masons. Hence, this study aims to compare membership in contemporary lodges to traditional observance lodges in terms of civic engagement. The remainder of the literature review covers additional reasons why we might expect to see differences in civic engagement among lodges, namely on the basis of age, education, and group size.

Hence, a dichotomy has emerged within the Masons in response to their decline in membership. In CLs there is a focus on raising membership numbers via lowering requirements. The TOLs represent a reaction against the development of CLs, stressing a renewed focus on higher standards for membership. This quantity versus quality dichotomy has possible implications for social capital and civic engagement among the Masons. Hence, this study aims to compare membership in contemporary lodges to traditional observance lodges in terms of civic engagement. The remainder of the literature review covers additional reasons why we might expect to see differences in civic engagement among lodges, namely on the basis of age, education, and group size.

The development of CLs was, in part, due to an attempt to appeal to a younger, faster paced generation. Putnam (2000) claimed that the decline in American civic engagement is largely a result of a change in generational mindset concerning volunteerism (Rotolo and Wilson 2004). Putnam (2000: 132) claimed that the "long civic generation" was highly active in civic engagement. This volunteer mentality was shaped by the Great Depression and World War II (Putnam 2000). Putnam (2000) purported that post WWII generations are less volunteer minded, less civically involved and more individualistic.

Rotolo and Wilson (2004) researched Putnam's generational hypothesis by analyzing data from the National Longevity Survey. He could only analyze the responses of women since only women were asked questions concerning volunteering during their preretirement years (Rotolo and Wilson 19 2004). The study showed that Putnam's (2000) assertion that current generations are less likely to volunteer is incorrect (Rotolo and Wilson 2004). To the contrary, the study found that younger participants contributed more hours of volunteering than older, retired participants (Rotolo and Wilson 2004). The study also found that the type of volunteering done by current generations is different. That is, older generations participated in 'traditional' forms of volunteer activity, such as church attendance and club memberships. Younger generations, the baby boomers of the civil rights era, were more prone toward political activism type volunteering (Rotolo and Wilson 2004). Hence, studies show that younger generations do not necessarily have less volunteer activity; rather, they have different types of volunteer activity. Hence, it is likely that age leads to differences in the amount and type of civic engagement among Masons as well. Because CL membership may be younger on average than that of TOLs (due to recent recruitment efforts targeted at younger generations), this may also contribute to differences in the type and quantity of civic engagement among members of the different lodge types.

Civic Engagement and Education

Traditional Observance Lodges place a heavier emphasis on the amount and type of educational experience received by Masonic members. Numerous studies indicate that there is a strong relationship between the level of one's education and his or her level of political or civic engagement (Wolfinger and Rosenstone 1980; Coleman 1988; Schultz 2002). Rotolo and Wilson (2004) noted that younger generations have higher levels of education and this may be the reason why he found that younger individuals were actually not less engaged than their older counterparts.

Hillygus (2005) analyzed responses from the Baccalaureate and Beyond longitudinal survey in order to analyze the relationship between education and civic engagement. Hillygus (2005) found that both level and type of education were related to level of individual civic engagement. Those respondents who had higher scores on verbal aptitude tests and those who received civic or social related higher education were more likely to be civically engaged (Hillygus 2005).

Therefore, education may influence differences in level of civic engagement among the Masons. Members with lower levels of education may be less civically engaged than those with higher levels of education. In addition to the level of education a person has, the field in which they receive a degree also likely influences their civic engagement. Given the emphasis on social issues within the humanities and social sciences, it might be expected that persons with degrees in these fields would be more civically engaged than people with degrees in other fields. Therefore, Masons with degrees in humanities and social sciences may be more civically engaged than Masons with degrees in physical sciences or business. Given the greater emphasis on education within TOLs, especially education specifically related to civic engagement and knowledge, it is expected that members of TOLs will have higher levels of education and be more heavily drawn from the humanities and social science fields than members of CLs.

Civic Engagement and Group Size

Not only do TOLs place a greater emphasis on traditional sources of education, TOLs also claim that the quality of Masonic civic education (within the lodge) is higher within TOLs. One factor that affects the quality of civic education within the lodge is group size (Lodge of Nine Muses No. 1776 2010; MRF 2010). Because TOLs tend to be smaller or cap their membership at around 70 members, it is argued they are in a better position to provide quality education to their members (Lodge of Nine Muses No. 1776 2010; MRF 2010). CL lodges can be well over 300 or 400 members in size. TOLs maintain that once a lodge has reached a certain size, the individual's lodge experience and contributions are lowered.

Studies show that group size affects the level of the individual's contribution and experience in relationship to the group's goals and activities. Studies indicate that the larger the group size, the lower the level of most individuals' participation in the group. This phenomenon is known as "social loafing" (Goodman 1986; O'Leary-Kelly, Martocchio, and Frink 1994; Shepperd 1995). Shepperd (1995) noted three reasons for this negative association between group size and individual contribution, namely that individuals feel that their contributions are unnecessary, unrewarded and too costly.

Group size may also impact civic engagement through its impact on governance. Barakso (2005) studied the National Organization of Women (NOW) and its relationship to civic engagement. NOW, like the Masons, is a democratically structured membership organization. Barakso (2005) found that the democratic practices of the organization fostered higher levels of civic engagement by its members. Both CLs and TOLs, like NOW, elect their leadership and vote on key organizational issues (GLoTx 2011; Hollingsworth 2011; UGLE 2011). However, TOLs claim that the size of group affects the ability to know and elect quality leaders. Specifically, TOLs claim that smaller groups, as opposed to the larger CLs, foster a better leadership selection process, which in turn leads to greater civic engagement. Therefore, TOLs which emphasize having a smaller, closer knit group, may have higher levels of civic engagement among their membership.

Summary

Putnam's theory of social capital, founded in the works of Tocqueville, serves as a foundation for numerous studies on civic engagement and social capital. The Masons are a civic organization that publically claims to support civic engagement and democratic concepts, concepts that are replete throughout social capital theory and civic engagement studies. The decline in membership for civic organizations over the past several decades has also impacted the Masons. Their response to these declines—the development of both CLs and TOLs—has important implications for the civic engagement of Masons.

The contrast in philosophy of these two types of lodges is also thought to be reflected in membership differences in terms of age, level and type of education, and group size. All of these factors may impact civic engagement. This study looks at each of these factors by utilizing an online survey of members of three different Masonic lodges in Colorado, one TOL and two CLs of different sizes. The foregoing review leads to the following hypotheses:

1. CL members will be less civically engaged than TOL members.

2. Age will be positively associated with civic engagement among Masons.

3. CL members will be younger on average than TOL members.

4. Younger Masons participate in different types of civic engagement than older Masons.

5. Level of education will be positively associated with civic engagement among Masons.

6. CL members will have lower levels of education than TOL members.

7. Masons with degrees in humanities and social science will be more civically engaged than those with degrees in other fields.
8. CL members will be less likely to have degrees in the humanities and social sciences than will TOL members.

9. Size of lodge will be negatively associated with civic engagement among Masons.
[...]

FINDINGS

Participant Characteristics

Participants in the survey consisted of 39 Masons. Fourteen participants were from the Traditional Observance Lodge (TOL) and a combined total of 25 participants came from the Contemporary Lodges (CL). Eight respondents claimed dual membership in both a TOL and a CL and were asked to answer lodge specific questions for each type of lodge (two appropriately labeled spaces were allotted for each question). Length of membership ranged from four months to 60 years with a mean of 19.8 years. Thirty-five of the participants were Master Masons and three reported being either Fellow Craft or Entered Apprentice Masons.

Of the participants, 10 have less than a Bachelor's degree, 14 hold only a Bachelor's degree, and 11 hold a post graduate or professional degree. The highest number of respondents report that their degree or field is in business (12), nine are in physical science, six in Social Science, and eight report having a degree in an "other" field. Participants ranged in age from 24 to 93, with an average age of 54.9 years of age.

Lodge Characteristics

The primary distinction used in this thesis is between TOL and CL lodges. It is therefore important to verify that differences that are assumed to characterize these lodges are supported by the data. TOL lodges focus on putting a cap on their membership numbers as a mechanism for ensuring a quality, rather than quantity, experience. The survey results confirm a difference in size between the TOL and CL lodges. The TOL reported membership size ranged from 20 to 224 members, with an average size of 75.1 members, which incidentally is the approximate reported size 24 for TOL lodges throughout the country. CL membership size ranged from 40 to 250 members, with an average of 118.3 members. While my use of the TOL/CL terminology may not have been perfectly clear to respondents (causing them to occasionally misrepresent which lodge they were a part of), the means here do indicate a smaller size membership for TOL lodges.

Since TOL lodges reportedly place higher emphasis on education, it was expected that TOL members would be more likely to be expected to compile or present a paper about Masonic education or experience. Again, the data confirm this distinction. Of the TOL respondents, 50% reported that they were expected to compile or present a Masonic paper. Of the CL respondents, only one person reported an expectation to compile or present a paper on a Masonic topic.

It was further expected that it would take TOL members on average longer to advance to the next blue lodge degree compared to their CL counterparts; this was confirmed by the data. Over one half (54%) of TOL members reported that it takes six months or longer for a member to advance to the next blue lodge degree. Of the CL members, only 14% reported that it takes six months or longer for a member to advance to the next blue lodge degree.

It was also expected that TOL membership dues would be higher than CL membership dues. Once again, the data support this distinction. The dues reported for TOL members ranged from $72 to $400 per year with an average of $270 per year. CL members reported membership dues ranging from $10 to $156 per year with an average membership dues amount of $113 per year.

Based again on the notion that TOL membership has heightened expectations, it was assumed that TOL members would more likely be expected to attend meetings of their lodge before advancing to the next blue lodge degree than CL members. Indeed, 67% of TOL members responded that they were expected to attend lodge meetings before advancing to the next degree. Only 25% of CL members reported that they were expected to attend lodge meetings before advancing to the next degree.

Finally, it was anticipated that TOL lodges would be more likely to hold meetings for the sole purpose of Masonic education than CL lodges. Of the TOL members polled, 75% reported that their lodge had held a meeting for the sole purpose of education or research within the past six months. Of the CL members polled, 57% reported that their lodge had held a meeting for this purpose within the past six months. In summary, the data suggest that all of the indicators used to distinguish TOL and CL lodges in terms of their emphasis on quality of experience are accurate.

Hypothesis 1: CL members will be less civically engaged than TOL members.

To test this hypothesis, respondents were first asked to evaluate whether they thought their Masonic affiliation had impacted their participation in civic activity. Of all of the respondents, 59% reported that their membership in Masonry helped increase their participation in civic engagement while 36% reported that their Masonic affiliation did not increase their level of civic engagement activity. Roughly equivalent proportions of both TOL and CL members reported that Masonic affiliation had no effect on their civic engagement: 36% of TOL members and 39% of CL members.

This hypothesis was examined further through the use of the full civic engagement scale. The average score of civic engagement for CL and TOL members was roughly the same ($t = -.394$, $p = .696$). The average CL score for the civic engagement scale was 24.9 (std. deviation = 9.94) while the mean score for TOL members was 25.9 (std. deviation = 5.74). Thus, the data suggest that this hypothesis is not supported.

Hypothesis 2: Age will be positively associated with civic engagement among Masons.

A correlation test between age and the full civic engagement scale was used in order to test this hypothesis. The test demonstrated a slight negative association between age and civic engagement among Masons ($r = -.098$, $p = .579$). While insignificant (due to small sample size), this negative correlation may indicate that younger Masons are equally if not more involved civically than their older counterparts, a notion that runs counter to the hypothesis.

Hypothesis 3: CL members will be younger on average than TOL members.

In order to test this hypothesis the average age of CL and TOL members was compared ($t = 1.586$, $p = .123$). The average age of CL respondents was 58.8 years old (std. deviation = 19.25) while the average age of TOL respondents was 49.4 (std. deviation = 13.02). These exploratory data imply that this hypothesis is not supported.

Hypothesis 4: Younger Masons participate in different types of civic engagement than older Masons.

In order to test this hypothesis a correlation test was used with age and each civic engagement sub scale. Age was not significantly correlated with the civic activity sub scale ($r = -.024$, $p = .893$), the electoral activity sub scale ($r = .039$, $p = .029$) and the civic voice sub scale ($r = .043$, $p = .011$). There was a statistically significant negative association between age and the electronic activity sub scale (r = -.552, p <.01). This indicates that younger Masons appear more likely to engage in electronic civic activity than older Masons. Thus, the limited exploratory data suggest that this hypothesis may be supported.

Hypothesis 5: Level of education will be positively associated with civic engagement among Masons. In order to gauge if level of education was positively associated with civic engagement the mean levels of civic engagement for those with at least a Bachelor's (four year) degree were compared to the mean levels for those with less than a Bachelor's degree (t = -.525, p = .603). Masons with less than a Bachelor's degree scored an average of 24.5 (std. deviation = 6.69) on the civic engagement scale while those with a Bachelor's degree or higher scored an average of 26.2 (std. deviation = 9.29). This indicates a possible positive association with level of education and civic engagement among Masons. Therefore, the data suggest that this hypothesis may be supported (the limited sample size precludes adequate significance testing).

Hypothesis 6: CL members will have lower levels of education than TOL members. In order to test this hypothesis the level of education was compared between CL and TOL respondents (chi-square = .244, p = .970). The comparisons indicated that 43% of CL members had earned a four year degree and an additional 29% of CL members earned a graduate/ professional degree. Among TOL members, 36% reported having a four year degree with an additional 36% reporting a graduate/professional degree. Therefore, this hypothesis appears to be supported, (again, limited sample size precludes adequate significance testing).

Hypothesis 7: Masons with degrees in humanities and social sciences will be more civically engaged than those with degrees in other fields. To test this hypothesis, the average civic engagement scale score was compared for Masons whose degree or field is in the social sciences/humanities versus Masons whose degree or field is not within the social sciences/ humanities (t = -.088, p = .930). Masons reporting having a degree or being in a non-social science/humanities field scored an average of 25.7 (std. deviation = 8.72) on the civic engagement scale while those within social science/humanities scored an average of 26.0 (std. deviation = 8.53). Given the very small differences in these means, this hypothesis does not appear to be supported.

Hypothesis 8: CL members will be less likely to have degrees in the humanities and social sciences than will TOL members. To test this hypothesis the type of degree (social science/humanities versus other) obtained by participants was compared between CL and TOL members (chi-square = 2.146, p = .143). The findings indicated that 29% of TOL members reported having a degree or being in the field of social science/ humanities compared to 10% of CL members. Thus, the data suggest that this hypothesis may be supported (as before, limited sample size disallows adequate significance testing).

Hypothesis 9: Size of Lodge will be negatively associated with civic engagement among Masons. To test this hypothesis the mean of civic engagement was compared for each lodge polled, the TOL lodge, a small CL lodge, and a large CL lodge (F = .770, p = .471). The mean for the TOL was 25.9 (std. deviation = 5.74) and the mean for the small CL was 26.5 (std. deviation = 10.80). The much larger size CL lodge had a mean of 22.0 (std. deviation = 7.89). This indicates a possible trend that as size of lodge increases the level of civic engagement among lodge members decreases. Thus, the hypothesis appears to be supported (although limited sample size precludes adequate significance testing).

DISCUSSION

This exploratory study aimed to examine civic engagement in America. This was done by using an exploratory analysis of the response by the Masons, a unique civic organization, to a decline in its membership in America. Specifically, this study explored possible differences in two approaches taken by contemporary Masonic organizations, namely the CL approach and the TOL approach. In addition to expectations with regard to differences in age, education and group size, a key hypothesis of this study was that each of these approaches would result in different levels of civic engagement among members.

Survey data from three lodges in Colorado were used to address the study's expectations. Since the survey data were limited by low response, leaders from each lodge were asked, via e-mail, follow up, interview-style questions that paralleled the study's hypotheses. Where relevant, their responses are incorporated in the following discussion to either counter or support results from the survey.

The first hypothesis addresses the core issues of this study, stating "CL members will be less civically engaged than TOL members." The data suggest that this hypothesis was not supported. It was expected that a TOL environment and focus on education would foster more civically minded and engaged members. The results demonstrated that the vast majority of respondents (nearly 60%) felt that their membership in Masonry increased their level of civic engagement. As one young Worshipful Master of his lodge put it, "I definitely think being a Mason increase(s) our awareness of community volunteerism. I think that the idea is that many of us have led a selfish life for most of our lives due to societal pressures." This statement indicates that Masonry overall may influence its members to be civically minded and active. It is noteworthy that Putnam (2000) argued that younger generations in America are developing an atomistic, individualistic mindset and behaviors which he considers dangerous to American democracy.

The statement; "the idea that many of us (younger members) have led a selfish life for most of our lives due to societal pressures," seems to directly support this claim by Putnam (2000) that American culture may be, in some ways, influencing younger generations, and in this case younger Masons, to perceive that they have a more individualistic mindset than older Masons.

While the average level of civic engagement for TOL members was slightly higher than CL members, there was not a statistically significant or substantively meaningful difference in overall civic engagement between CL and TOL members. In addition to having a limited number of survey responses (which increases the difficulty of finding statistically significant differences), a possible reason for this may be because Masonry, in general, tends to attract people who are already civically engaged. That is, of those polled, 95% reported volunteering for civic groups at some point in the past, with 79% having volunteered with civic groups (other than the Masons) within the past year. […]

Hypothesis 1 tested overall level of civic engagement between CLs and TOLs but did not account for the quality or type of civic engagement. It can be speculated that there is a difference in the specific types and/or quality of civic engagement between CL and TOL members. While the survey data cannot provide information about the quality (or extent of) civic engagement, it appears that there may be important differences in the types of civic engagement for CLs and TOLs. Although not statistically significant, CL members scored higher, on average, in terms of the civic activity subscale (CL mean = 5.9, standard deviation = 2.20; TOL mean = 4.9, standard deviation = 2.71). TOL members, on the other hand, scored higher on each of the remaining subscales. For electronic activity, TOL members had a mean of 2.3 (standard deviation = 1.14) and CL members had a mean of 1.8 (standard deviation = 1.54). For electoral activity, TOL members scored a mean of 10.4 (standard deviation = 2.50) and CL members scored a mean of 10.3 (standard deviation = 4.04). For civic voice activity, TOL members scored an average of 8.4 (standard deviation = 3.34) and CL members scored 7.0 (standard deviation = 4.73). Further study would be needed in order to see if type of lodge impacts the type, and especially, the quality of civic engagement.

The second hypothesis stated that older Masons would be more civically engaged than their younger Masonic counterparts. The results suggest that this hypothesis is not supported and in fact implied a slight trend opposing it. That is, there was a slight negative correlation between age and civic engagement. This runs counter to Putnam's broader societal claim that younger generations are less civically engaged than older generations in America. The findings for the second hypothesis are further corroborated by statements made by lodge leadership in their responses to follow-up questions.

For example, one lodge leader states; "Being in the younger category I think that a lot of what the older members are in lodge for is very different than the younger group. The younger members tend to seek more networking opportunities where the older members are uninterested in this." The key phrase in this quote is "networking opportunities." This language suggests that younger Masons are in fact seeking to connect with other individuals and groups. This is supported by another lodge leader who stated: "I like (that) several of our younger members have received help along the way through life via foster homes and the like and would like to give back in some way while building relationships along the way." This supports the claim that civic engagement increases social capital, which in turn cultivates more civic engagement, and that younger members are seeking to be civically engaged.

Another reason that the findings indicate that younger Masons polled are not less (and possibly more) civically engaged than older Masons could be related to the findings of hypothesis 4. Hypothesis 4 states; "younger Masons participate in different types of civic engagement than older Masons." The data seemed to indicate that younger Masons were more likely to be involved in social media networking, like Facebook or blogging, than older Masons. Therefore, it is possible that younger Masons are not less civically engaged than older Masons but rather participating in different types of civic activity. This was also demonstrated by Rotolo and Wilson (2004).

Hypothesis 3 stated that CL members would be younger on average than TOL members. It was thought that CL members would be younger than TOL members because CLs have generally lowered requirements for membership in order to make it easier for younger potential candidates to join. The findings suggest that this hypothesis is not supported. In fact, the findings indicate a possible trend that TOL members are considerably younger than CL members. Statements provided by lodge leadership may provide insight as to why this is.

The TOL leader stated: "younger Masons are looking for an experience rather than just a social club . . . older Masons tend to like the social aspect." CL leaders stated that younger Masons were seeking networking and relationship building opportunities as quoted above. Thus, based on these statements, it can be speculated that certain aspects of TOLs may attract younger members because their unique environment and focus on education are more in line with the expectations that younger potential members have concerning Masonic membership. Further study would be required to explore this possibility.

It appears that level of education is positively associated with civic engagement among Masons, as stated in hypothesis 5. This finding parallels other studies that find that the higher one's education, the more civically engaged they are likely to be (Wolfinger and Rosenstone 1980; Coleman 1988; Schultz 2002). Yet, all of the lodge leaders stated that they "did not think education background affected one's involvement in Masonry." However, the TOL leader stated that: "the educational background may affect a Mason's ability to learn the deeply esoteric aspects of Freemasonry. This is not to say that backgrounds other than liberal arts are not able to understand the mysteries of Freemasonry."

What is interesting here is that all three lodge leaders agree that any members, despite their education background, can be active in their lodge and civically engaged. However, the TOL leader notes that education background, specifically, level and type may be positively associated with one's ability to grasp deeper aspects of Masonic experience and education. This may lend credibility to the idea that type of education may impact type of civic engagement and not necessarily overall level of civic engagement. Again, further study is required to better understand this possible dynamic.

It was expected, according to hypothesis 6 that "CL members will have lower levels of education than TOL members." Further, it was expected in hypothesis 8 that "CL members will be less likely to have degrees in the humanities and social sciences than will TOL members." The findings tend to support both of these expectations. However, it was expected that those with degrees in humanities and social sciences would be more civically engaged (hypothesis 7). The findings suggest that this is not the case.

It is interesting that TOLs have a higher rate of members with graduate degrees and seem to attract more individuals with degrees in humanities and social sciences. This would seem to indicate that TOL members would be more civically engaged than the CL members surveyed, which, as previously stated, is not supported by the findings. This may indicate that Masonry has some type of nullifying effect for its members in relation to their level/type of education and level of civic engagement. In other words, despite one's educational background, simply being a Mason may impact civic engagement. It may also indicate that, as already noted, Masonry may tend to attract those who are already civically engaged. It may also be, as noted previously, that educational background impacts the quality or type of civic engagement rather than the overall level of civic engagement. Further study is required to substantiate these speculations.

Hypothesis 9 states that, "size of lodge will be negatively associated with civic engagement" and appears to be supported by the data and statements provided by lodge leadership. One CL leader stated: "I do feel that size of lodge impacts the participation in lodge events; however it is not simply the number of members, but number of active members." A leader from the other CL stated: "It is my personal opinion that Lodge size does matter greatly with a Lodge of say fifty members . . . it's easier to stay in touch with the members, keep track of them and each member feels a greater need for everyone to contribute for the better good." The TOL leader stated: "This small number allows members to get to know each other better. Since all members are relatively close, participation in Lodge events is greater." The statistical data along with these quotes support social loafing theory as discussed earlier, with members of larger lodges being less active on average than members of smaller lodges. This further suggests that a small lodge tends to foster or attract more civically engaged Masons.

CONCLUSION

Social capital and more specifically civic engagement are considered crucial for the existence and perpetuation of democracy in America. Tocqueville (1838) and more recently Putnam (2000) have conducted major studies on civic engagement. Putnam's (2000) highly cited and studied works demonstrate a strong, positive relationship between civic engagement and democracy in America. The Masons are an organization that has existed in America since prerevolutionary times. It is commonly thought that historical actions by Masons were instrumental in the development of democratic practices in America. The Masons are unique in American history and in relation to American civic engagement because they have existed from the colonial era through the present and teach their members to be civically minded and active. Further, they have influenced the development of other civic groups in America. This study explored civic engagement in America by examining the reaction by the Masons to a decline in its membership, an issue that has afflicted numerous civic groups and activities in American society. The reaction to decline in membership among the Masons has led to the development of two types of Masonic lodges in America, CLs and TOLs. This study compared these lodges in relation to their member's civic engagement activities and background characteristics.

It is interesting that TOLs have smaller sized lodges, have younger members, and have more members with degrees in humanities and social sciences. All of these factors, with the exception of age, would indicate that TOLs have a higher level of social capital and therefore produce more civically minded and civically engaged members. That, however, was not supported by this study. TOL members were slightly more civically engaged than CL members in this study, but the limited survey response precludes any definitive statement in this regard.

108

It can be stated that Masons, at least the ones polled in this study, are very civically engaged. For example, nearly 90% of respondents reported having voted in local, state, and federal elections within the past four years, well above national averages. Nearly all respondents are members of other civic groups outside of Masonry. The question then becomes, does Masonry produce civic engagement or does Masonry attract people who are already civically engaged? It would be interesting to further explore the degree to which TOL members are engaged in different types of civic engagement than CL members, and what implications those differences may have for Masonry and American culture in general, if they do in fact exist. However, due to the limitations of this study, further study is needed to explore this possibility.

A chief limitation of this study is the low survey response rate (~10%). This low response rate may seem to conflict with the emphasis Masons place on voluntary activity and the importance of scientific research. However, it should be noted that while Masons stress the importance of civic engagement, we also place a high value on the privacy of Masonic lodge information. It could be that guarding privacy outweighed participating in the survey for most potential participants. Another explanation may be that only the most active members participated in the survey. By active members, I mean those who attend lodge meetings on a regular basis and stay highly informed on lodge functions. The results here would then further support the idea that smaller lodges have a higher level of participation among members. That is, approximately 30% of TOL members participated in the survey and around 10% of the lodge membership participated from the CL lodges. In any case, future research, as is the case for other secretive organizations of interest to Sociologists, will need to take this high value of privacy into account before we can make more definitive conclusions.

REFERENCES

Barakso, Maryann. 2005. "Civic Engagement and Voluntary Associations: Reconsidering the Role of the Governance Structure of Advocacy Groups." Polity 37 (3): 315-334.

Bessel, Paul M. 2012a. "Freemasons and the U.S. Declaration of Independence." Freemasons. Retrieved August 6, 2011. (http://bessel. org/declmas.htm).

Bessel, Paul M. 2012b. "Prince Hall Masonry Recognition." Freemasons. Retrieved June 19,2012. (http://bessel.org/masrec/phamap.htm).

Boggs, Carl. 2002. "Social Capital as Political Fantasy." Pp. 183-202 in Social Capital, edited by Scott L. McLean, David A. Schultz, and Manfred B. Steger. New York, NY: New York University Press.

Coleman, James S. 1988. "Free Riders and Zealots: The Role of Social Networks."Sociological Theory6 (1): 52-57.

East Denver Lodge No. 160. 2011. "Ancient Free and Accepted Masons of Colorado: Traditional Observance." Retrieved August 26, 2011. (http://www.eastdenver160.com/).

Fried, Amy. 2002. "The Strange Disappearance of Alexis de Tocqueville in Putnam's Analysis of Social Capital." Pp. 21-49 in Social Capital, edited by Scott L. McLean, David A.Schultz, and Manfred B. Steger. New York, NY: New York University Press.

George Washington Masonic Memorial, The. 2011. "George Washington, the Mason." Retrieved August 7, 2011. (http://gwmemorial. org/washingtonTheMason.php).

GLoTx. 2011. "The Grand Lodge of Texas: Freemasonry and the American Revolution." Retrieved August 6, 2011. (http://www. grandlodgeoftexas.org/search/node/U.S.%20declaration%20of%20 independence).

GLoV. 2011. "The Grand Lodge of Ancient Free and Accepted Masons of Virginia. History of the Grand Lodge of Virginia." Retrieved November 17, 2010.http://www.grandlodgeofvirginia.org/history/index.htm).

GLoV. 2012. "The Grand Lodge of Ancient Free and Accepted Masons of Virginia: Appendant Bodies of Freemasonry." Retrieved June 19,2012. (http://www.grandlodgeofvirginia.org/appendant_bodies/index.htm).

Goodman, Paul. 1986. Designing Effective Work Groups. San Francisco, CA: Jossey-Bass.

Hillygus, D. Sunshine. 2005. "The Missing Link: Exploring the Relationship Between Higher Education and Political Engagement." Political Behavior 27 (1): 25-47.

Hollingsworth George. 2011. "Masonic Tourist: Living History, Freemasonry in Williamsburg, VA." Ancient and Accepted Scottish Rite. Retrieved July 21, 2011(http://scottishrite.org/journal/july-august-2011/ living-history/).

Independent Order of Odd Fellows, The. 2009. "History of Odd Fellows: Why the Name OddFellows?". Retrieved August 16, 2011.(http://www. ioof.org/history/history_california.html).

Kaufman, Jason and David Weintraub. 2004. "Social Capital Formation and American FraternalAssociation: New Empirical Evidence. The Journal of Interdisciplinary History35 (1):1-36.

Lichterman, Paul. 2006. " Social Capital or Group Style? Rescuing Tocqueville's Insights on Civic Engagement. "Theory and Society 35 (5/6): 529-563.

Lodge of Nine Muses No. 1776. 2010. "Free and Accepted Masons of The District of Columbia:Members." Retrieved August 26, 2011. (http:// www.lo9m1776.org/Membership.html).

LVX Lodge No. 848. 2009. "Free and Accepted Masons of California: About: who we are."Retrieved August 22, 2011. (http://www.calodges. org/no846/about.html).

Moffrey, Robert W. 2001. "The Rise and Progress of the Manchester Unity Independent Order of Odd Fellows." The Isle of Man.org. Retrieved August 7, 2011. (http://www.isle-of-man.com/manxnotebook/ history/socs/odf_mdly.htm).

MRF. 2010. "The Masonic Restoration Foundation: The Foundation." Retrieved August 20,2011. (http://traditionalobservance.com/).

O'Leary-Kelly, Anne M., Joseph J. Martocchio, and Dwight D. Frink. 1994. "A Review of the Influence of Group Goals on Group Performance." The Academy of Management Journal37 (5): 1285-1301.

Putnam, Robert D. 2000.Bowling Alone: The Collapse and Revival of American Community. New York, NY: Simon and Schuster.

Rotolo, Thomas and John Wilson 2004. "What Happened to the 'Long Civic Generation'? Explaining Cohort Differences in Volunteerism." Social Forces82 (3): 1091-1121.

Schultz, David A. 2002. "The Phenomenology of Democracy: Putnam, Pluralism, and Voluntary Associations." Pp.74-98 in Social Capital, edited by Scott L. McLean, David A. Schultz, and Manfred B. Steger. New York, NY: New York University Press.

Shepperd, James A. 1995. "Remedying Motivation and Productivity Loss in Collective Settings." Current Directions in Psychological Science 4 (5): 131-134.

St. John's Lodge No. 1. 2011. "Ancient York Masons: History of Freemasons." Retrieved August 4, 2011. (http://www.stjohns1.org/ portal/).

Tocqueville, Alexis De. 1838.Democracy in America. London, England: Saunders and Otley.

Tufts University. 2006. "Civic Engagement Quiz." Retrieved December 21, 2010. (http://www.civicyouth.org/PopUps/Final_Civic_Inds_Quiz_2006.pdf).

UGLE. 2011. "The United Grand Lodge of England: History of Freemasonry." Retrieved November 17, 2010. (http://www.ugle.org.uk/).

Wolfinger, Raymond. E., and Steven J. Rosenstone. 1980. Who Votes? New Haven: Yale University Press.

THE FOUR MASONIC ELEMENTS

By Dr. David E. Stafford

(Editor's Note: some pictures or illustrations have been edited out of this paper)

Freemasonry has been described as being veiled in allegory and illustrated by symbols. Through the centuries of time, the allegories and symbols of the Craft have been obscured and made only partially recognizable to the meanings they held in antiquity. The ritual, as used in each jurisdiction, has evolved and been pruned in such a manner that within the work are blurbs and sections that have little meaning in its present context or to modern Masons; however, it is within these scattered gems of purpose that a studying Mason may find great enlightenment. One such portion of the ritual maybe found with the seemingly haphazard mentioning of the four elements, water, fire, earth, and air, usually found at the conclusion of the stereoptics in the Entered Apprentice Degree. Their inclusion within the ritual seems a little awkward and misplaced, but as will be discussed within this paper, other Masonic rites use the elements in a more prominent and pronounced manner than does the common York/American Rite system. In either event, it raises the question as to why the classical elements of water, fire, earth, and air were ever introduced to the rituals of the Craft.

The American Ritual

The rituals used in American lodges are for the most part similar. Most US grand lodges confer a derivative of the Preston/Webb ritual. There are but few exceptions. The variations within the majority of the rituals adopted by US grand lodges are usually only associated with verbiage and sequence of events. Although this ritual does illustrate the importance of our Mother Earth, the elements are not mentioned at all within the ritual of the First Degree as practiced under the auspice of the Grand Lodge of Tennessee, to whom the author owes allegiance. The following is from the 2003 edition of the Tennessee ritual, and it is very similar to Indiana's (Taylor, 1975).

112

Our ancient brethren, we are told, served their Master with Freedom, Fervency, and Zeal, which are symbolically illustrated by chalk, charcoal, and clay. For there is nothing more free than chalk, which upon the slightest touch leaves a trace, nothing more fervent than charcoal, which when properly ignited melts the most obdurate metals, and nothing more zealous than Clay or our Mother Earth, for from the earth we came and unto the earth we must all inevitably return.

Another common passage found within the Preston/Webb Rituals pays little to no attention to freedom, fervency, and zeal and a larger amount to the elements. McCoy (1855) and Sickels (1868) are both examples. It will later be shown how this passage is extremely similar to the wording of an ancient Greek authority. On page 98 of Daniel Sickels' 1868 edition of The General Ahiman Rezon and Freemason's Guide the ritual reads:

Our Mother EARTH alone, of all the elements, has never proved unfriendly to man; the bodies of water deluge him with rain, oppress him with hail, and drown him with inundations. The air rushes in storms, prepares the tempest, and lights up the volcano; but the earth, ever kind and indulgent, is found subservient to his wishes. Though constantly harassed, more to furnish the luxuries than the necessaries of life, she never refuses her accustomed yield; spreading his path with flowers and his table with plenty; though she produces poison, still she supplies the antidote, and returns with interest every good committed to her care; and when at last he is called upon to pass through the "dark valley of the shadow of Death," she once more receives him, and piously covers his remains within her bosom: this admonishes us that from it we came, and to it we must shortly return.

The Freemason's Guide to the Symbolic Degrees (Reed, 1968) welds the two afore quoted passages together in the Entered Apprentice Degree. The combination is found in the same place within the ritual, after the discourse on the virtues and before the charge. The same is done in the Kentucky Monitor, the Louisiana Masonic Monitor, New York's monitor, and the Masonic Manual of Missouri (Carman, 1952; Huckaby, 1927; Missouri, 1952; Pirtle 1990). The Tennessee ritual includes the latter discourse not in the First Degree but within the Masonic Funeral Service. These three variations appear to be the most common within the York/ American Rite Craft Degrees as practiced in the United States. Within the context of the entire discourse of the third section of the First Degree, the inclusion of references to any of the elements seems a little out of place. The reason for the inclusion of any of these variations has been questioned for at least the last sixty years, and it would probably be safe to say for much longer (Barbour, 1946; Wells, 1947).

In various rites and obediences, a candidate for the First Degree of Freemasonry must endure a series of trials to prove his sincerity and character. Perhaps the trial that would be familiar to most American Freemasons would be the chamber of reflection, for many have experienced a similar trial in at least one of the concordant bodies. According to Mackey (1927), the use of the chamber of reflection prior to the Entered Apprentice Degree is common in the French and Scottish Rites, neither of which are widely practiced within the regular grand lodges in the United States. The chamber of reflection will be discussed and examined later in this work.

In a 1946 article found in The Philalethes, Barbour discusses the use of the four elements as trials in the Rite of Misraim. Pike and Cummings (2001) spent a great deal of time in combating the legitimacy of this rite and that of Memphis in the United States. They clearly assert the spuriousness of the Rite of Misraim, the Rite of Memphis, and the one formed through the irunion. All three of these are frequently, albeit perhaps harshly, called Masonic bastards (Stevens, 1899). The modern irregularity of the rite in the United States is without question; however, according to Barbour, Marc Bedarride, a former Grand Master of the Rite of Misraim in France and accused charlatan, recorded a "quite lengthy, detailed, and perhaps imaginary" description of the rite's trials. The description includes the proselyte being caused to transverse an underground cavern, pass between two engulfing flames, to wade a swift current of water of unknown depth without extinguishing his torch, being exalted through space where his light is darkened by a blustering gust of air, and finally being hastened into a "chamber of horror" just outside of the room where he is to be initiated. This is a dramatic account of this obedience's trials, but it illustrates the passage presumably required of those seeking enlightenment within the French Rite of Misraim, at least in spirit.

Although extremely unpractical within the setting of a lodge hall, the description corresponds, in narrative, to the trials detailed within Pike's (1993)Porch and the Middle Chamber: Book of the Lodge and Ambelain's (2006)Freemasonry in Olden Times: Ceremonies and Rituals from the Rites of Mezaraim and Memphis1. At least one current Rite of Memphis and Misraim in the United Statesis purportedly in the use of Ambelain's work (Brother Methodius, personal communication, July 15,2008). Robert Ambelain is of Martinist fame. It appears the ritual is more heavily influenced by esoteric and occult thought than is mainstream American Masonry; however, the ritual shows a very strong similitude to Pike's Craft Ritual. This is not surprising since both find their origin developing within France. Ambelain's ritual warrants a review by anyone who is interested in variations of Masonry.

Pike's Craft rituals are not widely known within the United States. He revised the Scottish Rite version of the Craft Degrees not to be worked within the halls of a lodge but instead as a perquisite reading for a York Rite Mason venturing through the Scottish Rite's fourth through the thirty-second degrees (Pike, 1993). This objective explains the frequent digressions within Pike's ritual to clarify the differences between York Rite work and Scottish Rite work. It was believed by Pike that the rites contrasted so greatly in presentation that the York Rite Mason would not be able to fully understand the lessons within the Scottish Rite without some exposure to its Craft Degrees. Pike believed that after familiarizing himself with the Scottish Rite version of the Three Degrees that a candidate for the "higher" degrees would not be puzzled by their order. To provide one example of the differences between the American/York Rite Craft ritual and that of the Scottish Rite, within the American/York Rite ritual, the ruffians are apprehended and punished before the conclusion of the Third Degree. This is not so within the Scottish Rite workings of the degree, it is not until the completion of the10thdegree, or Elu of the Fifteen, that the fullness of retribution is paid to the ruffians. The following is an examination of Pike's use of the elementals within the First Degree.

Pike's "Blue Degrees" and the Elements

Pike's version of the First Degree involved four tests or trials by the elements. The first trial experienced by the candidate is that of earth and involves the Chamber of Reflection. The following three trials are known as "The Journeys" and are made up of circumambulations around the lodge with various barriers and experiences to encounter. Each journey is accredited with an element, ordered air, water, and fire. The following is a description of each trial paraphrased from Pike's (1993) Porch and the Middle Chamber: Book of the Lodge and (1996)Esoteric Work of the 1st through 3rd Degree, According to the Ancient and Accepted Scottish Rite.

Chamber of Reflection

The first trial of a candidate for the first degree is that of earth. The proselyte is delivered to the lodge by the individual who recommended him to Masonry. The profane is promptly left in the hands of a conductor, who blindfolds the proselyte and leads him about the lodge in the allusion of descending into a deep pit or catacomb. The candidate is then seated on a stool and turned over to the instruction of the preparer. The room is prepared with images of death and despair. Present also is a cup of water, apiece of bread, and dishes of salt, sulfur, and mercury. The proselyte is left to explore the crypt and answer four written questions before him. Each question is related to the candidate's duties he owes to himself, fellow creatures, his country, and his creator, respectfully. He is instructed that once he has answered the questions and followed all instructions to ring a bell signifying his completion. The preparer observes the candidate through a hidden wicket, and when the candidate begins to answer the questions a disturbance outside of the chamber occurs. The proselyte hears chains rattling, cries, and a loud explosion followed by silence. Once he answers the questions, the candidate is required to write a will, drink the water, eat the bread, and reflect upon the salt, sulfur, and mercury. The latter substances' connections to alchemy are explained. They are described as being representative of man's three fold being: body, mind, and spirit. The salt is a reminder of the endless cycle of the dead becoming part of the living. The smoke from burning a particle of sulfur represents good and evil thoughts. The mercury with its inability to be easily divided into portions is representative of the spirit in simple oneness. After the proselyte has completed his tasks, the preparer blindfolds him and leads the candidate back through the path from whence he arrived at the chamber.

The First Journey

The first journey represents trial by air. During this journey the candidate is conducted three times around the lodge. He is caused to traverse objects on the floor as if passing over rocks and through hollows. All the while, sounds of thundering and loud clasps are made about the journeyman. The candidate is stopped by the Junior Warden and made to make an alarm by striking the Junior Warden on the left shoulder three times. At this point, the candidate is given a light electric shock accompanied by a loud clasp of thundering sounds. After answering the Junior Warden's brief interrogation, the first journey is completed. The candidate is then informed that the element air is a representation of vitality or life. In a deeper explanation, the trial by air is said to be emblematical of the whims of life and more especially the quality of tolerance and progress from a terrestrial to a celestial state of being.

The Second Journey

The second journey represents trial by water. During this trial, the candidate is conducted three times around the lodge. After each circumambulation, the candidate's right hand is dipped in a laver of water. The lodge is completely silent during the journey. After the third revolution, the candidate is stopped at the Senior Warden and made to make the regular alarm by striking him three times on the left shoulder. It is explained to the candidate that baptism by water is a symbol of purification and used by the Essenes and John the Baptist. It is to be a reminder to the candidate that all men must be driven by a desire to serve his fellow creature; otherwise, when fortune finds opportunity to invest him with rank and honor, he will serve himself and not the people who gave him opportunity.

116

The Third Journey

The third and last journey represents trial by fire. To best convey the venture taken by the candidate on the third journey, much of the description to follow is taken directly from Pike's (1996) Esoteric Work of the 1stthrough the 3rd Degree. According to the Ancient and Accepted Scottish Rite. The profane is once again conducted three times around the lodge. "He is continually exposed to heat, which is produced by means of along metallic tube, having at one end a mouth-piece and at the other aspirit-lamp, surrounded with wire-gauze. The tube contains lycopodium or arcanson powder, which, blown upon the spirit-lamp, inflames, and passes through the wire-gauze, making a hot flame. Torches may be used, with cotton saturated in alcohol, and powered with lycopodium, which rains out in flames when the torch is shaken" (p. 12). The candidate is to clearly feel the heat from the apparatus but not be burned. Upon the last circumambulation, the candidate is stopped by the Worshipful Master and caused to make an alarm on the Worshipful Master's shoulder just as before. The candidate is then taught that through the baptism of both water and fire, he is symbolically free from all sin and vice. He is then instructed that the flame teaches all Masons to aspire for perfection and labor with aspiration, ardor, and zeal (very similar to freedom, fervency, and zeal in the York/American ritual).

Ambelain's Ritual and the Elements

Ambelain's Freemasonry in Olden Times contains two separate sets of rituals, those of the Rite of Memphis and the Rite of Mizraim. It is suggested that any reader with an interest in various Masonic Craft rituals spend some time in studying these unique and beautiful systems. There are some interesting differences between Ambelain's ritual and that of Pike. The first variation of Ambelain's ritual from that of Pike's is the absence of mercury, sulfur, and salt from the Chamber of Reflection. The order of the trials is different in the rituals. In Ambelain's ritual the order is water, air, and fire (air, water, and fire in Pike's).

The first journey includes the candidate being conducted around the lodge with immense noise and harassment. At the conclusion of the circumambulation, at the Junior Warden, the candidate's hand is plunged into pure water for purification.

The second journey being a test of air, the candidate is lead around the lodge in silence, although obstacles are still present. Stopping at the Senior Warden, the Master of Ceremonies blows three times on the candidate's forehead.

The third and last journey is a trial by fire. The candidate is once again conducted around the lodge and stopped by the Worshipful Master. The Master of Ceremonies takes the right hand of the candidate and passes it three times through the flame of a lit candle.

These differences are only presented to give the reader a little broader view of how the elements are used in different rituals. It is hoped that a reader with an interest will seek out these rituals and read them fully, for they all have a great many gems of purpose to impart to the Masonic student.

The Elements in Literature

Throughout antiquity and the more modern era, the four elements have been included in literature ranging in genre from poetry and science fiction movies to academic works on conservation and physics (Besson, 1997; Laurie, 1929; Rupp, 2005; Sylvester, 1979). Of particular interest is that the majority of the passage concerning the four elements from Sickel's monitor, and various other York Rite renditions, is lifted from the ancient writings of Pliny the Elder. Practically word for word, depending on translation, the Sickel and McCoy monitors recite Pliny's discourse from Book II, Chapter 63 of Naturalis Historia (Laurie, 1929; Pliny, 1987). Naturalis Historia was completed around the year 77 AD, and it is considered to be one of the largest works, consisting of 37 books, to have survived from the era of the Roman Empire until today (Rupp). Pliny reads:

It is the earth that, like a kind mother, receives us at our birth, and sustains us when born. It is this alone, of all the enemies around us, that is never found an enemy to man. The floods of waters deluge him with rains, oppress him with hail, and drown him with inundations; the air rushes on in storms, prepares the tempest, or lights up the volcano; but the earth, gentle and indulgent, ever subservient to the wants of man, spreads his walks with flowers, and his table with plenty; returns with interest every good committed to her care, and though she produces the poison, she still furnishes the antidote, though constantly teased more to furnish the luxuries of man than his necessities, yet even to the last, she continues her kind indulgence, and when life is over, she piously hides his remains in her bosom.

Joshua Sylvester (1979) in the robust work The Divine Weeks and Works, first published in 1621, presents a stanza that is very reminiscent of Pliny the Elder's writing. All four elements are referred to; however, it is the earth that is most revered. Pay particular attention to the commonality of line 467:

459: *The Earth receives man when he first is born:*
460: *Th'Earth nurses him; and when he is forlorn*
461: *Of th'other Elements, and Nature loaths-him,*
462: *Th'Earth in her bosom with kind buriall cloaths-him.*
463: *Oft hath the Aire with Tempests set-upon-us,*
464: *Oft hath the Water with her Floods undon-us,*
465: *Oft hath the Fire (th'upper as well as ours)*
466: *With wofull flames consum'd our Towns and Towrs:*
467: *Onely the Earth, of all the Elements,*
468: *Unto Mankind is kind without offence:*
469: *Onely the Earth did never it displace*
470: *From the first seat assign'd it by thy grace.*

In recent literature, the four elements have received considerable attention for their prominent inclusion in Dan Brown's (2000) work Angels and Demons. The book fictionally connects the four classical elements with the practice of an Illuminati conspiracy and assassin. On page 360, Brown depicts what he refers to as The Illuminati Diamond, an artistic creation forming the words Earth, Air, Fire, and Water into a square figure. The novel repeatedly mentions political figures' connections to Freemasonry and Freemasonry's supposed and illusionary connection with symbols such as the eye within a triangle and the Great Seal of the United States. In the fictional novel, bodies are found branded with an anagram of one of the four elements somewhere on their person. There are numerous other references in literature that compare favorably to the subject at hand; however, it would be beyond the scope of the current focus to expound more fully upon them. Let it be made very clear, the similarity of our modern ritual to these older works does not in any waypoint to the age of the fraternity; yet, it does indicate that the ideas and thoughts propagated within the lodge are linked to those of a more ancient time.

The History of the Four Elements

It would now be prudent to briefly examine the development of the four elements. Throughout all ages and even today, man sought to identify the prima materia, prime matter or primary material, of all substances (Vorhand-Ariel, 1998). The debate over the fundamental building blocks of all material is as old as civilization itself. It was the group of thinkers belonging to the school of natural philosophers, in the sixth century BC, who first begun to seriously debate the elements (Rupp, 2005). Thales is accredited with being the first to develop a theory of elements. He proclaimed that water was the most basic of all elements and that all things were made of some variation of this base material. The debate continued for centuries. Anaximander, Thales's student, proclaimed that air wasthe basic unit of matter. Heraclitus proclaimed the simplest element must be fire, and Xenophanes asserted that all things were made of the fundamental element of earth (Rupp).

It was Empedocles (494-435 BC) who is accredited with combining the theories of his predecessors and developing a four-prong theory of the elements, although Buddha's teachings of the four elements pre-date Empedocles'. In Tetrasomia or Doctrine of the Four Elements, Empedocles postulated that all things were made up of various combinations of earth, air, fire, and water. According to Rupp (2005), the development of a set of basic elements was not exclusive to Greece, the cradle of Western Thought. Japanese and Hindu traditions taught of a five element belief. Both taught the four classical elements and a fifth element akasha, aether, or the void which explains the unseen, spiritual influences of life and nature. Within the Greek philosophy, the presence of a fifth element, ether, was regularly discussed and debated. Aristotle added a fifth element he called aether, later it was termed quintessence. The peoples of India developed a three element theory and those of China a five element theory. The Indian theory contained fire, water, and earth to which the Chinese added wood and metal. The Indians later expanded the theory to include air.

The Greek thought of the four classical elements has been greatly confused in modern time. When the Greeks debated and discussed the four elements they did not have a physical substance in mind. When the Greeks discussed earth, they did not necessarily intend for it to be taken as soil; although it would often be represented as such. The four classical elements more readily referenced physical states of being. The following excerpt clearly explains:

For Aristotle, matter (hyle), inert and shapeless by itself, gained its shape and properties by the action of form (morphe) which could be expressed by such factors as hot, cold, dry and humid, giving in turn, by their combination, four elements: earth (cold and dry), water (cold and humid), air (hot and humid) and fire (hot and dry). The elements were eternal and indestructible and by synthesis (chemical reaction), mix is (mechanical mixing) orkrasis (dissolution) gave birth to different substances whose properties depended solely on the contents of each element. (2)

During the Middle Ages, Western thought was stifled and oppressed. Alchemy and the study of the four elements was overcome in the Western world by superstition and blind faith in the church; however, in the East, the same period was a time of great growth in science, literature, philosophy, and overall intellectual achievement. Alchemy "developed in close relation with metallurgy andmedicine" within the Islamic Arabian-Persian world (Tramer, Voltz, Lahmani, & Szczepinska-Tramer, 2007, p. S6). It was during this time that the Arab scholar Abu Musa Jabir ibn Hayyan, more readily known as Gerber (720-780 AD), lived and worked (Tramer, Voltz, Lahmani, & Szczepinska-Tramer). Gerber was profoundly interested in alchemy, and he believed that all metals were made up of a combination of sulfur and mercury.

Gerber's sulfur-mercury theory was expanded by Al-Razi (850-940 AD), a Persian physician, to include salt (Rupp, 2005).

"In the late Middle Ages (12-14th centuries), alchemy was studied by such eminent personalities as Albertus Magnus—Albert von Bollstadt (1193-1280), professor of philosophy and theology at the Universities of Cologne and Paris, or Arnaldus de Villanova (1235-1313), rector of Montpellier University" (Tramer, Voltz, Lahmani, & Szczepinska-Tramer, 2007, p. S6). In the 16thCentury the Greek theory of elements and the Arabian three elements were combined. "Paracelsus (Phillip vonHohenheim, 1493-1541) determined that, though the Greek four were indeed the fundamental components of all matter, earth, air, fire, and water in turn were composed of the three Arabic 'principles,' mercury, sulfur, and salt" (Rupp, p. 23).

The classical elements composing of either four or five elements dominated philosophic, scientific, esoteric, and mathematical thought from Empedocles through Socrates, Plato, Aristotle, Gerber, Paracelsus, and their dominance began to weaken in the middle of the 17thCentury with the scientific research of Robert Boyle. Boyle's (2008). The Sceptical Chymist signaled the end of the four elements dominance in science. For the next 100 years, the dominance of alchemy and the four elements over Western society waned. The death of alchemy has been symbolically represented by Antoine Lavoisier, who listed thirty-three elements classified as gases, metals, non-metals, or earths in his 1789 dissertation entitled Elementary Treatise on Chemistry (Donovan, 1996; Rupp, 2005). From this point, the number of identified elements increased at a steady if not amazing rate (Rupp). It is noteworthy to mention, however, that even today the classical elements and alchemy are used in astrology, esoteric thought, and several other occult philosophies.

It was not uncommon for cultures to connect their belief of the elements with other basic knowledge such as colors, seasons, symbols, directions, religious iconography, virtues, or planets, attributing one of each to a specific element. The Greeks were no different from their global companions. The Pythagoreans, those philosophers who followed the teaching of Pythagoras, had a natural affection for numbers, and to them, the world of nature and reality seemed to divide itself nicely into units of four. They observed four elements, "four prime faculties, four societies, four seasons, four ages of man, and four parts of living things" (Rupp, p. 12). It was the Pythagoreans who are accredited with developing four of the Seven Liberal Arts and Sciences, the quadrivium: arithmetic, geometry, astronomy, and music (Stahl, Johnson, & Burge, 1991). Hippocrates took this fascination with four and connected the four elements to his four essential fluids of the human body (yellow bile, black bile, blood, and phlegm).

Ginsburgh (1995) asserted that the Hebrew people saw a correspondence between the four classical elements and the letters of the Tetragrammaton. In Ginsburgh's view water correlates with Yod, fire with Heh, air with Vav, and earth with the final Heh. Bogdan (2007), Castells (2005), and Ozaniec (2005) concurs that there is a correlation between the name of God and the four classical elements. According to some writers, the four classical elements when corresponded with the Tetragrammaton may be further associated with the four senses, four evangelists, four angels ruling over the corners of the world, and the four triplicities (Castells (2005); Goldstein, 1990; Labriola &Simmonds, 2000; Ozaniec). "A triplicities is a set of three zodiacal signs: there are four triplicities in all, each of which is associated with one of the four elements" (Goldstein, p. 1). Bogdan stresses that the illustration of this connection is displayed more fully or clearly in rituals of the Order of the Golden Dawn than they are within Freemasonry. Kabalistic philosophy is deeply rooted within the study of the Tetragrammaton. The Tetragrammaton and Kabalistic philosophy are repeatedly seen within the degrees of the Scottish Rite, including the Craft Degrees (Hutchens, 1995a; Hutchens, 1995b).

Within the American/York Rite's "higher" degrees is a very clear example of how units of four were associated with each other. In the Royal Arch Degree, the candidate is caused to pass through four veils, each representing one of the principal tribes of Israel. The first veil represents the tribe of Dan and is represented by a blue banner bearing the representation of an eagle. The second veil represents the tribe of Rueben and is represented by a banner of purple bearing the representation of a man. The third veil represents the tribe of Ephraim and is represented by a scarlet banner bearing the representation of an ox. The fourth veil represents the tribe of Judah and is represented by a banner of white bearing the representation of a lion. According to Royal Arch and early Christian tradition, each of the four veils is said to represent one of the four Christian Gospels of John, Matthew, Luke, and Mark, respectively. The representations of the eagle, man, ox, and lion are further described as corresponding to four astrological symbols of the Zodiac: Scorpio, Aquarius, Taurus, and Leo, respectively.

In Morals and Dogma, Albert Pike (1956) connects even more units of four with the four representations on the Royal Arch's banners while discussing the twenty-eighth degree of the Scottish Rite. On page 791, Pike presents an illustration connecting the eagle with azoth and air; the man with mercury and water; the ox with salt and the earth; and the lion with sulfur and fire. Pike continues to explain how the Zohar further connects each illustration on the banners with an angel: the lion with Michael; the ox with Gabriel; the eagle with Uriel; and the man with Raphael.

Alchemy

The four classical elements are intimately related to the ancient science of Alchemy. The discipline, not unlike Freemasonry, is divided into two denominations: material and spiritual or operative and speculative (Tramer, Voltz, Lahmani, & Szczepinska-Tramer, 2007).

Alchemy was very en-vogue with the thinkers of the Renaissance (14-17 centuries) but fell out of popularity with the rise of the "rational and critical philosophy of the enlightenment" mind (Tramer, Voltz, Lahmani,& Szczepinska-Tramer, p. S6). It is not to be assumed however that alchemy instantaneously disappeared from the social, political, and scientific scenes.

Whereas the material practice of alchemy sought to explain and manipulate the physical world, the spiritual alchemist sought to use the terminology, science, and ideas of the material to explain the psychological, spiritual, and sociological existence of man. Alchemy was interested in transmuting one thing into another. Of course the most widely known idea of alchemy is the search for a technique of converting base metals into silver or gold; however, within the spiritual denomination of alchemy there was a search to return man to a pure oneness with the divine creator. Although the once prominent theories of alchemy lost position in the open scientific worldview, its spiritual half found refuge in the esoteric beliefs of organizations such as Freemasonry and the Rosicrucian movement. The traditional quest within alchemy was transmutation, or change, into another substance or form (Von Franz, 1980). This quest in relationship to the four elements can still be found within The Elemental Trials of Freemasonry.

Before going farther, it would be advantageous to explore what connections the framers of the Craft have with alchemy and its practice. The beginnings of Freemasonry are shrouded in mystery. At what point the operative lodges transformed into an organization accepting men of stature and prestige is blurred; however, it is generally accepted that Elias Ashmole, Robert Moray, and Christopher Wren were among the first to transcend the barriers and become speculative or accepted Masons (Beresiner, 2004; Koltko-Rivera, 2007; MacNulty, 1998). It is also noteworthy that all three of these men were founding members of the Royal Society. It is possible that more members of the Royal Society were Freemasons; however, even of the three afore mentioned, Wren and Moray are occasionally questioned as Freemasons. It is not suggested that the Royal Society has any connection in origin to Freemasonry; however, it is implied that both organizations developed during the transition from the Renaissance to the Enlightenment thought. It is also suggested that the men in both organizations probably shared similar interests, one of which being alchemy and the rapidly developing science of chemistry.

Elias Ashmole was born on the 23rdof May 1617 at Lichfield, Staffordshire England (Beresiner, 2004). Ashmole was made a freemason in 1646 within the lodge at Warrington (Koltko-Rivera,2007). From an early age, Ashmole found a fond interest in esoteric teachings. He had a passion for botany, astronomy, and alchemy. He became fast friends with William Backhouse, a notedal chemist, and this relationship was so strong that, according to Koltko-Rivera, Ashmole became the alchemical successor to Backhouse. Ashmole also had an interest in Rosicrucianism; however, there seems to be no record of him ever being a participant in Rosicrucian activities. Ashmole published several works with esoteric and alchemic connotations including Fasciculus Chemicus, Theatrum Chemicum Brittannicum, and The Way of Bliss (Beresiner; Koltko-Rivera; MacNulty, 1998).

Robert Moray was born March 6, 1609. He was initiated into Masonry in 1641 at the Lodge in Edinburgh. Moray was a lover of hermetic philosophy and alchemy, and he was the patron of Thomas Vaughn, an active alchemist (MacNulty, 1998;McGregor, 2005).

Christopher Wren was born October 20, 1632 (McGregor, 2005). It is believed that Wren was initiated into Freemasonry in May 1691 as evidenced by John Aubray's Naturell Historie of Wiltshire. There is little to no firm evidence, however, to substantiate the assertion that Wren was definitely a Freemason. His interests in intellectual endeavors, however, are unquestionable. Wren was raised in an Anglican family that leaned towards the Royalist agenda during the civil unrest in England. He was educated at an early age by his father and Reverend William Shepherd. He attended Westminster School for several years. Following a change in prosperity, the Wren's resided with William Holder. It was here that Wren was exposed to William Scarburgh, a physician. Scarburgh was a member of a small group of thinkers who met weekly to discuss such topics as alchemy, physics, astronomy, statics, and the like. Wren was allowed to attend many of these meetings. Christopher Wren was among the first twelve founding members of the Royal Society and served as president for several years (McGregor, 2005).

The Elemental Trials as Illustrations of Transmutation

"According to Aristotle, the prima material combines with the four qualities of coldness, dryness, heat, and moisture, to develop into the four elements. He believed that manipulating these qualities would change their elemental composition, resulting in transmutation" (Vorhand-Ariel, 1998, p. 110). Within alchemy, it was believed that the elements could be manipulated in order to produce a mystical substance, or the philosopher's stone. This belief in manipulating what was found in nature into a supernatural substance, transmutation, transposed itself into the philosophy of Rosicrucian and Freemasonry. Nowhere within all of Freemasonry is this more clearly evident than in the elemental trials.

Earth

Within the York/American Rite, it is taught that "our Mother EARTH alone, of all the elements, has never proved unfriendly to man". The ritual further "admonishes us that from" the earth "we came, and to it we must shortly return". The element of earth represents man's alpha and omega, his beginning and his end. Man's body was molded together with the dust of the earth and water. His mortal temple was an earthen clay vessel into which God breathed air through his nostrils to transmute him into a living soul. The first living man was Adam, who is recognized within Masonic tradition and myth as being the first Freemason. The name Adam comes from adamah, meaning earth or ground (Mackey, 1927; Vorhand-Ariel, 1998). It may be of interest to mention here that according to Jewish law it is unlawful for a corpse to be cremated. One explanation for this edict is that a body that is returned to the earth "is capable of bringing forth new life"; whereas, a body that is turned to ash through burning by fire represents complete destruction (Kaplan, 1990, p. 149). The Jewish religion and Freemasonry both teach that man is an eternal being that awaits resurrection after death. It is therefore proper that man's body be laid under the solemn clods of clay as a symbol of his awaiting resurrection and return to the endless cycle of life. It is appropriate that the Masonic rituals of elemental trials begin with the candidate being placed deep within the earth. It may be interpreted as a symbol of his beginnings. When the profane candidate leaves the Chamber of Reflection, he is born anew and prepared to receive instruction as a tabula rasa or blank slate (Zeldis, 2008).

Air

The word wind is intimately related to the word spirit. It has already been mention that it was breath that made man a living soul. God breathed air into man's nostrils to make him a free moral agent, made in the likeness of the Godhead, Father, Son, and Holy Ghost. The Arabic word ruchand the Hebrew word ruachare words meaning both soul and wind (Kaplan, 1990; Vorhand-Ariel, 1998). Jung (1989) asserted that it was only natural for man to associate air with the soul, for life begins with a baby's first gasp for breath and ends with a man's last struggle to breathe. When a man breathes his last breath and the air leaves his body, his soul vacates the carnal clay vessel and transmutes to eternal reward or damnation.

Water

The second journey within Pike's ritual is the trial by water. In Western, alchemist, and Jewish thought, water has a deep rooted connection with creation, birth, and renewal (Rupp, 2005; Vorhand-Ariel, 1998). The first two elements mentioned within the Christian and Jewish Bible are earth and water. In modern science, it is taught that life on earth began within the primordial ooze of the ancient oceans.

The process of a mother delivering a baby is signaled by the breaking of her water. Through a study of ancient civilizations, it is found that the earliest societies developed on the banks of the fertile rivers of life: the Tigris, the Euphrates, the Nile, the Indus, and the Yellow Rivers; thusly, it might be suggested that water has always been a source of life and fertility to the human race (Kaplan, 1990; Vorhand-Ariel, 1998).

Water has played a vital part in the rituals of the world's major religions. Although much of the Christian world views baptism and ceremonial immersion as a rite isolated within their practice, mikvahis a ritual bath practiced in Judaism (Vorhand-Ariel). The Holy Scriptures of the Jews require followers to participate in a ceremonial immersion in order to purify themselves. Causes for such a requirement are varied but include women after childbirth or menstrual cycles, converts to Judaism, and the Cohen Gadolor High Priest before performing a ceremony representing the people(Vorhand-Ariel). Within the Muslim religion, practitioners are required to go through purification by water before prayer. It is thereby a safe assertion that the washing of the body in water is an ancient symbol of the purification of the immortal soul and the carnal vessel. Its use within the Craft is no different. The alchemist used water as a sign of transmutation and purification. Before setting to work, the alchemist prepared his tools and vessels by immersing and washing them in a bath of water (Vorhand-Ariel). Perhaps it is only fitting for the first degree of Freemasonry to purify and prepare a candidate for the Ancient Mysteries within a symbolic water baptism.

Fire

To the ancient Hebrews and to alchemists, fire was the most active of the elements. It was fire that served as a catalyst. According to Vorhand-Ariel (1998), "Heraclitus regarded fire as an agent of transmutation and as a symbol of renewal, representing light, spirit, the sun, radiance, and purification" (p. 111). The alchemists used fire, as well as water, as a source of purifying their tools. The alchemist and metallurgist both used fire to refine metals and make them pure. It separates the base from the precious metal (Tramer, Volts, Lahmani, & Szczepinska-Tramer, 2007). Fire was used by them to transform a crude convoluted mixture into a separated collection of base and precious metals. "The Zohar says the flaming sword [referred in Genesis as being placed east of the Garden of Eden] symbolizes the trials with which God overwhelms man that he may be purified and restored to the way of goodness" (Vorhand-Ariel, 1998, p. 112). It might be mentioned here that the tiler's sword was traditionally wavy in shape to represent the sword placed in the Garden of Eden(Lawrence, 1999; Mackey, 1927). As afore mentioned, fire is a symbol of renewal and has been since time immemorial. Perhaps one of the best images of this is the traditional phoenix. The phoenix is a mythical bird that after an extensive life combusts into flames and is reborn from its owns ashes. In Thus Spake Zarathustra, Nietzsche (2003) wrote, "You must be willing to burn in your own flame: how could you become new unless you had first become ashes?" (p. 49). The ancients implemented a trial by fire perhaps similar to Pike's variation of the Entered Apprentice degree. Perhaps it is a reminder to the neophyte that he must set aside or destroy his old image of life and self to receive the teachings of Freemasonry and become a new and better creature.

Conclusion

At the onset of this work, the question was raised concerning the inclusion of the classical four elements within the Entered Apprentice Degree in various ritual variations. The examination of this topic has transcended time passing through the studies of religion, philosophy, and history. In the study of the elements, the topic of alchemy repeatedly revealed itself. It has been illustrated how the discipline of alchemy dominated the religious, political, scientific, and social aspects of human existence. Tramer, et al. said of alchemy, "alchemy, an integral part of the medieval world-view, was doomed to death by the spirit of enlightenment well before its official death which coincided with the appearance of the modern chemistry of Lavoisier and Dalton. [Now] Only its phantom is still alive" (p. S5). It is most probable that a very prominent place where alchemy is still shining is within Freemasonry. The early speculative Freemasons came from the ages of the Renaissance and the Enlightenment. It is without question that these patriarchs of the Craft were knowledgeable in both denominations of alchemy and their relationship with the four classical elements. It is proposed, and hopefully supported, that sporadic mentioning of the four elements within the York Rite system and the blatant use of the elements within the rites of continental Europe are direct decedents from the reign of alchemy in pre Enlightenment Europe. The early framers of the Craft, during the Renaissance, probably drafted the rituals to include the philosophies of spiritual alchemy that aligned with the spiritual needs and goals of the fledgling organization of Speculative Freemasonry.

Works Cited

1) For other rituals, reference Arturo de Hoyos' Rituals of the Masonic Grand Lodge of the Sun Bayreuth, Germany, Kessinger Publishing, 1997 and Hoyos and S. Brent Morris' Committed to the Flames: The History and Rituals of a Secret Masonic Rite, A Lewis Publishing, 2007.

2) Tramer, A., Voltz, R., Lahmani, F., Szczepinska-Tramer, J. (2007). What is (was) Alchecmy?,Acta PhysicaPolonica A, 112 (Suppl.), S5-S18.

Elements			
Water	Fire	Earth	Wind/Air
Zodiac			
Aquarius	Leo	Taurus	Scorpio
Gospels			
Matthew	Mark	Luke	John
Daniel's Vision			
Man	Lion	Ox/Bull	Eagle
Principal Tribes			
Reuben	Judah	Ephraim	Dan
Angels			
Raphael	Michael	Gabriel	Uriel
Alchemy			
Mercury	Sulfur	Salt	Azoth
Greek Gods			
Neptune	Vulcan	Juno	Jupiter
Hippocrates 4 Humours			
Phlegm	Yellow Bile	Black Bile	Blood
Platonic Shapes			
Icosahedron	Tetrahedron	Cube	Octahedron
Colors (Pike)			
White	Red	Black	Blue

(Barbour, 1946; Pike, 1956; Rupp, 2005; Wells, 1947)

References

Ambelain, R. (2006).Freemasonry in Olden Times: Ceremonies and Rituals from the Rites ofMizraim and Memphis.Adventures in Spirit Series/Robert Laffont, Translated by Piers A.Vaughan.

Barbour, P. P. (1946). The four elements,The Philalethes, 1(3).

Beresiner, Y. (October 2004), "Elias Ashmole: Masonic icon", MQ Magazine(11): 6–11

Besson, L. (1997).The Fifth Element. Columbia Pictures.

Bogdan, H. (2007).Western Esotericism and Rituals of Initiation. New York, NY: SUNY Press.

Boyle, R. (2008).The Sceptical Chymist. New York: BiblioLife.

Brown, D. (2000).Angels and Demons. New York: Pocket Books.

Carman, E. R. (1952).Monitor of the Work, Lectures and Ceremonies of Ancient Craft Masonry in the Jurisdiction of the Grand Lodge of Free and accepted Masons of the state of New York. New York, NY.

Castells, F. (2005).Arithmetic of Freemasonry. Canada: Templar Books.

Donovan, A. (1996).Antoine Lavoisier: Science, Administration and Revolution, New York:Cambridge University Press.

Ginsburgh, Y. (1995).The Alef-beit. Northvale, NJ: Jason Aronson Inc.

Goldstein , B., R. Bernard, D. Pingree (1990).Levi Ben Gerson's Prognostication for theConjunction Of 1345.Transactions, 80(6) The American Philosophical Society.

Huckaby, G. C. (1927).Louisiana Masonic Monitor. Grand Lodge of Louisiana: Louisville, KY.

Hutchens, R. R. (1995a).A Bridge to Light. The Supreme Council 33°, AASR, S.J..

Hutchens, R. R. (1995b).Pillars of Wisdom. The Supreme Council 33°, AASR, S.J..

Jung, C. G. (1989).The Collected Works of C. G. Jung (Vol. 14). Princeton, NJ: PrincetonUniversity Press.

Kaplan, A. (1990).Innerspace: Introduction to Kabbalah, Meditation, and Prophecy. Moznaim.

Koltko-Rivera, M. E. (2007). "The transmission of esoteric knowledge and the origins of modern Freemasonry: Was Mackey right?".Heredom, Volume 15.Washington, D.C.: The Scottish Rite Research Society.

Labriola, A. C. & Simmonds, J. D. (2000).Milton Studies. University of Pittsburg Press: Pittsburgh, PA.

Laurie, A. (1929).Fertilizers for Greenhouse and Garden Crops. The A. T. De La Mare Company: New York, NY.

Lawrence, J. T. (1999).Perfect Ashlar and Other Masonic Symbols. Kessinger Publishing.

Mackey, A. G. (1927).Encyclopedia of Freemasonry and its Kindred Sciences. Philadelphia, PA: McClures Publishing Company.

MacNulty, W. K. (1998). "Kabbalah and Freemasonry",Heredom, Volume 7. Washington, D.C.: The Scottish Rite Research Society.

McCoy, R. (1855).The Masonic Manual. J. W. Leonard, Harvard University.

McGregor, M. I. (2005).The Life and Times of Sir Christopher Wren. (Retrieved from http://www.freemasons-freemasonry.com/christopher_wren_freemasonry.html).

Missouri (1952).Masonic Manual of Missouri. Grand Lodge, A.F. & A.M. of Missouri: USA.

Nietzsche, F. (2003).Thus Spake Zarathustra: A Book for All and None. New York: Algora Publishing.

Ozaniec, N. (2005).The Kabbalah Experience: The Practical Guide to Kabalistic Wisdom. Sterling Publishing Company: UK.

Pike, A. (1956).Morals and Dogma of the Ancient and Accepted Scottish Rite of Freemasonry. Richmond, VA: D. H. Jenkins, Inc.

Pike, A. (1993).Porch and the Middle Chamber: Book of the Lodge. Kessinger Publishing.

Pike, A. (1996).Esoteric Work of the 1stthrough the 3rdDegree. According to the Ancient andAccepted Scottish Rite. Kessinger Publishing.

Pike, A. & W. L. Cummings (2001). The spurious rites of Memphis and Misraim,Heredom,Volume 9. Washington, D.C.: The Scottish Rite Research Society.

Pirtle, H. (1990).Kentucky Monitor. Grand Lodge of Kentucky, F&AM.

Pliny the Elder (1987).Naturalis Historia. Teubner, New York, NY.

Rupp, R. (2005).Four Elements: Water, Air, Fire, Earth. Profile Books, New York, NY.

Sickel, D. E. (1868).The General Ahiman Rezon and Freemason's Guide. New York: Masonic Publishing and Manufacturing Company.

Stahl, W. H., Johnson, R., & Burge, E. L. (1991).Martianus Capella and the Seven Liberal Arts. Volume I: The Quadrivium of Martinanus Capella. New York: Columbia University Press.

Stevens, A. (1899).The Cyclopedia of Fraternities. Hamilton, New York.

Sylvester, J. (1979).The Divine Weeks and Works. Oxford University Press.

130

Taylor, L. R. (1975).Indiana Monitor and Freemason's Guide. Most Worshipful Grand Lodge of Free and Accepted Masons of the State of Indiana.

Tennessee. (2003).Tennessee Craftsman or Masonic Textbook, 25thEdition. Most WorshipfulGrand Lodge of the State of Tennessee: Nashville, TN.

Tramer, A., Voltz, R., Lahmani, F., Szczepinska-Tramer, J. (2007). What is (was) Alchecmy?,Acta Physica Polonica A, 112(Suppl.), S5-S18.

Von Franz, M. (1980).Alchemy: An Introduction to the Symbolism and the Psychology. Toronto: Inner City Books.

Vorhand-Ariel, S. (1998).Alchemy and Jewish Mysticism: A Psychological Exploration of theirSymbolism, Art, and Practices. (Doctoral Dissertation, UMI #3008502) Pacifica Graduate Institute. Wells,

L. E. (1947). The elements,The Philalethes.

Zeldis, L. (2008). The Initiation in the Ancient Accepted Scottish Rite. The Journal of the Masonic Society, 1.

The "Nashville Days" of Andrew Jackson
By David Edward Stafford, Ed.D.

As most of you are aware, prior to becoming a state, Tennessee was part of North Carolina. In 1778, James Robertson and eight other men first scouted the Nashville area in hopes of establishing a settlement. The following year, Robertson returned with an estimated two hundred and fifty people to build a permanent settlement and prepare for their wives and families who were coming by boat with Colonel John Donelson. One of the interesting things about this trip is that the first people who came into the Nashville area, one being James Robertson, thought that it would be an easier track for their wives to come by flatboat. The men came by foot, their wives came by flatboat. In all reality they had it completely backward. It was much easier to come by foot, come through the gap, and then cross over the rough land. What happened when the ladies crossed over and came by flatboat is that many areas of the Cumberland River were not deep enough to support boat travel. You have to get off and carry the boats rather than actually stay on the flatboats and come all the way down. It was a very harsh and rugged trip for the ladies. They actually had a harder time with the Indians. The entire trip was longer, harder, and was much more disease ridden than the trip of the men, who thought they were taking the rugged route by foot.

After arriving in the Nashville area, the families entered into a social compact which was called the Cumberland Compact, and they named the settlement Nashborough. As we all know, it is not called Nashborough today. Instead, it is called Nashville. The reason Nashville had its name changed from Nashborough to Nashville is primarily due to the fact that "borough" is a British root word for city. Following the era of repeated hostility between the Americas and the British Empire, settlers and Americans did not want to be associated with the British. Being British was not something they celebrated. This was during the time of Post-Revolutionary war. Not wanting to be associated with the British, they changed the name from Nashborough to Nashville, which is very much a French name. As we look at society at the time, they were very fascinated with French culture. Even though they did not always associate with the French view of things, as we look at the mansions that were built and the homes as they were being furnished, they would most readily buy furniture from the French or Italians more so than they would from the British because they did not want anything that was associated with British culture.

In 1796, Tennessee became the sixteenth state in the Union. According to pop culture, the person who named or gave the suggestion for the name "Tennessee" was Andrew Jackson. The question is, was it possible that the name "Tennessee" was suggested by Andrew Jackson. The answer to that is no. The gentleman who actually made the suggestion was from Sumner County.

However, pop culture being what it is, it was much more popular to say Andrew Jackson suggested the name "Tennessee" than the unknown gentleman who actually suggested the name "Tennessee" for the state. Even today in school houses across Tennessee, teachers are telling students that Andrew Jackson came up with the name Tennessee. This is actually not true.

Nashville's location on the Cumberland River set it in a position to experience growth and prosperity. The availability of expedient transport for the day via steamboat provided Nashville with the ability to trade with Baltimore, Pittsburgh, Philadelphia, and New Orleans. Commerce in Nashville began to develop with banking, printing, publishing, and "king cotton." It is important for us to remember that Tennessee, and more especially Nashville, was part of a rugged frontier even up until 1850. In 1802, the population of Nashville proper was little more than five hundred people. In Davidson County, which covered a much larger area than what we think of Davidson County today, had probably no more than a couple of thousand people living in it. It is simple enough to say that if you lived in the general vicinity of Nashville, if you lived in the Middle Tennessee area, you had run across Andrew Jackson at least once in your lifetime.

The area of Middle Tennessee was very much rugged. As we look at the houses that were built and these great majestic mansions that were built during that time, and we walk through them today, in retrospect we get the idea of this grand gentry of people who lived there. In reality, it was not that way. They had nice furnishings and nice homes, but we have to remember that Tennessee, up until really the early 1900's, was a rough and rowdy place. It was not unusual to have shootings in the street. It was not unusual for brawling to just break out at any given moment. Society was very different from the romantic images that come to mind from touring the Hermitage. We think of Tennessee as being a very developed area, but just a hundred years ago it was full of back wood frontiersmen, saloons, trading posts, brothels, and various other un-reputable institutions.

Acquaintances of Jackson in the early Nashville time included James Robertson, who was the early father of the settlement. Charlotte Avenue that runs through Nashville is named after Robertson's wife, who served as a strong female leader among the band of families who forded the Holstein in traveling to the Nashville settlement of Nashborough.

McGavock Pike and McGavock High School, which is a very prominent, well known name in the Nashville area, were named after the McGavock family. David McGavock came to the Cumberland settlements in the late 1790's. The family is responsible, at least in lore, for the McGavock house in North Edgefield and Two Springs Mansion, which is a beautiful Italian Revival mansion.

Deaderick Street is named after George M. Deaderick who was a confidant and sometimes creditor of Andrew Jackson. Deaderick was Nashville's first banker. His bank had branches in Murfreesboro, Shelbyville, Gallatin, and Rogersville. An interesting story concerning Deaderick and Jackson has to do with Deaderick's marriage relationship with his wife, Polly. Deaderick and Polly began to have problems while Deaderick was in Knoxville on business. When he returned to Nashville, he found out that his wife, Polly, had been seen at several dance parties unaccompanied by her husband, which was quite a scandal in the day. She was not only at dance parties, but she had been seen playing cards with at least one single man at the card table. Today, we would think that was a typical, normal event for someone, whose husband who was out of town, to go to someone's house to play cards. But in the early 1800's, that was very scandalous, and it was a reason for divorce. Deaderick came home and he was quite upset with his wife, and thus the two became estranged. The person that Deaderick went to as broker to help restore union in the marriage was Andrew Jackson. We all know that Jackson had quite the temper. Why would you go to a man like Jackson to help reunite you with your estranged wife? The answer to this is that, although Jackson was a rough and rowdy man, he had a wife that he loved and adored.

Jackson was known for being a man who was very gentle to his wife. He had been accused on numerous occasions of being submissive to Rachel. When Deaderick needed help with his wife, he went to Andrew Jackson. One of the issues that we see in this whole debacle is that Jackson was very gentle with his wife, but Jackson was not gentle with Deaderick's wife when he goes to try to broker the reunion of these two wayward souls in this marriage. Polly accused Jackson of being ungentlemanly. This accusation was given no credit. What actually happened was that Jackson went to visit Polly and basically told Polly what her position as a wife was and told her that she needed to reconcile with her husband with no uncertain words. Polly took offense to Jackson's words and thus within a few months there was a filing for a divorce. At that time, divorce was not a simple task. During that time in Tennessee, a divorce required a vote by the full Tennessee Legislature. A bill had to be passed in order for you to gain a divorce. The legislature voted granting Deaderick and Polly a divorce. Deaderick also, following the War of 1812, held a massive reception for Jackson upon his return to Nashville.

Another gentleman, John Harding, was most assuredly accompanied with the General. Harding Place in Nashville is named after him. Also, Belle Meade Plantation in Nashville was Harding's home. Harding was a great lover of thoroughbreds. One of the favorite pastimes of Jackson's was horse racing. Jackson was a great lover of horses. He bred horses and also sponsored many races in the Middle Tennessee area.

Timothy Demonbreun was a French-Canadian trader who first lived in a curious old cave above the Cumberland River within the bluff of the West bank. He was a political leader in the Nashville area. Demonbreun, Jackson, and Harding all three had a huge interest financially in horse racing.

Nashville was not the only town that was greatly influenced by Jackson. Jackson also had law offices in Gallatin and Lebanon, which are Sumner County and Wilson County today. Jackson had great impact with the Knoxville and East Tennessee area as well. Jackson's first term in the legislature would have placed him in Knoxville. The Tennessee State Government was not originally seated in Nashville—instead the State Government met in Knoxville. Jackson was a regular visitor to the Knoxville area. In Gallatin, Jackson spent a lot of time at Wall Spring which was the home of his good friend and horse enthusiast, Colonel George Elliot.

Jackson migrated from the Waxhaw district of his youth to the frontier of North Carolina and spent some of those years in Knoxville. It became painfully obvious to everyone in the bustling little town of Knoxville that the town was not big enough for Jackson and his rival, "Ole Jack." "Ole Jack" was one manner in which Jackson referred to his elder statesman, John Sevier. Other names that Jackson had for John Sevier are probably not appropriate to mention in mixed company. Jackson and Sevier's relationship was extremely strained and difficult. It is absolutely amazing that the state of Tennessee in its size was able to hold both of these men.

As one story goes, Jackson was staying at a hotel in Knoxville and he decided to go to the tavern. When he arrived outside the lobby, he noticed John Sevier in a buggy in the street. Jackson immediately stepped into the street and began to curse the man in the buggy. The man began to yell back. There were shots exchanged and Sevier's buggy took off down the road. Jackson called for his carriage. Jackson gets into his carriage and the two men race through the bustling little Knoxville yelling curse words and strong names at each other. Finally, someone jumps into Jackson's carriage, calms him down, and talks him out of hunting down "Ole Jack" and killing him. One of the interesting things about their relationship is that John Sevier was twenty years Jackson's senior. They never could get along. In Jackson's mind, John Sevier was an older fellow who tried to "Lord" over Tennessee's heritage. In Sevier's mind, Jackson was a young whippersnapper who tried to take preeminence over his elder statesmen. These two men had a very strong battle between each other. One of the interesting things is that even today you still see a rift between Middle Tennessee and East Tennessee. Politically, those two factions of the state have been very dynamic.

Today, Tennessee is unified as a red state. Traditionally, that has not been true. Middle Tennessee has been very much led over the last one hundred years, not by the Republican Party but by the Democratic Party.

East Tennessee was a Republican stronghold. You had a strong political disagreement that stood between Middle Tennessee and East Tennessee that goes all the way back to these two men. Middle Tennessee was led by Andrew Jackson and East Tennessee was led by John Sevier. This hatred between these two men is still somewhat visible in Tennessee politics today. It is amazing when we look at Tennessee History to see how deep rooted those feelings have continued to be.

In Nashville, Jackson had a reputation as a land purveyor, attorney, businessman, and a socialite. Doctor Felix Robertson, son of John Robertson, has described Jackson as a cool, shrewd man of business. Let us not be confused with what socialite meant in the early 1800's in Nashville. Do not be confused with the socialites and debutantes of today with their white dresses and men dressed in their black suits. During Jackson's time, a socialite in Nashville was a man who participated in such activities as cockfighting, horse racing, gambling, card playing, billiards, drunkenness and the like. Such activities did not detract from your standing in the communities. In fact, if you were not a participant in those activities, your manhood was very much in question and you may have been called a dandy or a man who was not as manly as what he should be.

Jackson, along with his close friend and partner, John Coffee, after whom Coffee County is named, assembled as regular attendees at cockfights. On the Fourth of July in 1809, they organized and financed a major cockfight in Nashville. It is said that Jackson could be heard distinctly from the crowd, and I quote, "cheering his favorite bird with the loudest bolstering." He was a very flamboyant and "in your face" man.

If you ask people what they know about Andrew Jackson, their first response is that he was President of the United States. The second response is usually, "isn't he the one that was in the duel with a fellow?" The answer is yes, he was involved in at least two duels in his life, the most famous of which was with Charles Dickinson. The whole story of Charles Dickinson gives us a true reflection of what Middle Tennessee and the Tennessee frontier was like during Jackson's age.

Jackson and Coffee, being ever lovers of sports, developed a horse racing stable, field and track at the plantation at Clover Bottom in the Nashville area. Jackson had owned and operated a general store at Clover Bottom from 1804 to 1806. Jackson purchased a horse by the name of Truxton in Virginia. Truxton was trained by a slave in his early thirties by the name Dinwiddie. Dinwiddie had a reputation of being an excellent judge of horses and a marvelous trainer and breeder. An event was scheduled at Clover Bottom for November 1805. The event did not occur supposedly due to foul weather.

The second event was rescheduled for a few months later in 1806. It was advertised as, "the greatest and most interesting match ever to be run in the western country." The prize was three thousand dollars which, in the early 1800's, was a great sum of money. There was a match race between Jackson's Truxton and a horse by the name of Plowboy which was owned by Charles Dickinson's father-in-law. In case of forfeit, the remaining party was to receive eight hundred dollars. Plowboy was removed from the race and Jackson received eight hundred dollars on the day of the race. It seemed all was well.

The very interesting back story was, we really don't know if Truxton would have been able to run the race or not. Two weeks before the race, Truxton took a fall and tore a ligament in his hindquarter. It is very possible that Truxton was not going to be able to run but Jackson told Dinwiddie that "the damn horse will run regardless of what shape he's in." Truxton was going to run that race regardless. Jackson was not going to forfeit even if the horse had to be put down at the conclusion of the race. Plowboy was not able to run and, therefore, Jackson looks like the bigger man. Jackson's horse shows up, he receives eight hundred dollars, everyone's happy, end of story, so they thought.

A few months later, Charles Dickinson, who was a dandy of the day and had some questionable background himself, was drunk in a Nashville tavern. He was overheard making comments about Rachel Jackson's unsavory character. He also made a couple of comments about Jackson's business dealings, all of which the General was not very pleased with. Just in case some of you do not know the background between Jackson and Rachel, Jackson was raised a Presbyterian. In the frontier it was very common for Presbyterians to have what was called a common law marriage, meaning that, in the frontier, there were not a huge number of ministers, so you would have just a friend of yours to perform a ceremony. You considered yourself married and that's the way it was. Also in the frontier, it was not uncommon for women to be left without a husband. Their husband goes out on along hunt and a year later they never come back home. You don't know if the man is dead, abandoned his wife, or what. It was not uncommon during the frontier for a woman to end up having two husbands unbeknownst to her.

In the situation of Rachel, this was actually even a little bit more convoluted. Rachel was married to a man by the name of Robards. Robards had abandoned her. He was very abusive to her. She had requested a divorce and he had agreed. Rachel was under the understanding that he had gone to the State Legislature and they had voted for her divorce. She thought she was a single woman. She meets Jackson at her family tavern. They court and soon they are wed. They are wed with the traditional Presbyterian frontier marriage and they are considered married. A short time thereafter, they find out her divorce was never finalized. Her first husband had never sent the divorce through the State Legislature.

Jackson realizes he has been in a marriage that was not legitimized. Quickly they rush to get the divorce pushed through legislature. The divorce is solemnized and Jackson and Rachel are remarried. The marriage became completely legal and legitimate. That did not politically wash away those couple of years they had lived together when they were not legitimately married. That is the unsavory character that Dickinson was referring to. Jackson, being the man that he was, confronted Dickinson about his comments. Dickinson backed up very quickly and said, "General, I'm sorry. I apologize for my comments. I was drunk. I had way too much to drink. I was inebriated and that was my problem. I apologize for that." Jackson accepted his apologies in a true gentlemanly fashion and, once again, we thought the story was over.

A few months later, Dickinson is back in a tavern. He is drunk once again and his mouth begins to run again about the same things. Word gets back to Jackson and Jackson once again goes back to Dickinson. Only this time, instead of talking about Rachel's unsavory character, Dickinson begins to talk about the horse race. He talks about Jackson's having stolen his father-in-law's money because the race never took place. Even though Jackson received the money fair and square, Dickinson was accusing Jackson of having cheated to get the money. The General was infuriated. Once again, the General confronts Dickinson. Dickinson apologized again. For a third time, we are at a spot where we think all is well and fine. It probably would have remained that way had it not been for Jackson's friends and Dickinson's friends.

Jackson's friends, Sam Houston and John Coffee, continued to stir the pot. They did not let the situation die. They continued to run rumors with each other. There was a young lawyer in Nashville by the name of Thomas Swann. Thomas Swann stepped in, too, and gradually increased the hostility as well - only he did it on the side of Dickinson. Swann runs an article in the newspaper. In fact, he mentions Jackson as a liar. There were two things you did not do with Jackson. Number one, you did not say anything about his wife Rachel. Number two, you do not call him a liar. This began a series of newspaper articles going back and forth between Jackson and Swann. In the first article, Jackson accuses Swann and Dickinson of being base and cowardly. It is assumed that this would end the matter, but it did not. Dickinson had been hurried off to New Orleans by his friends in hopes that if he were in New Orleans, both men would calm down and this whole ordeal would be over. As soon as Dickinson returns to Nashville from New Orleans, he meets Jackson on the street. The two quickly begin to have words. The result was a duel. The two agree to meet for a duel. Jackson challenged Dickinson and Dickinson accepted. It was decided they would meet on Friday, May 30,1806, at Harris Mills on Red River in Logan County, Kentucky. In Tennessee, it was illegal to duel but in Kentucky, it was legal. Therefore, they crossed the state line into Kentucky. The two adversaries meet to settle the score.

Dickinson was an expert marksman. It was very much expected for Dickinson to kill Jackson in the duel. Jackson was very aware of Dickinson's reputation as an expert marksman and an expert dueler. Dickinson had been involved in several duels. Obviously since he was still living, he was good at dueling. Since Jackson knew this, he wore a coat that was three sizes too big for him. When Dickinson looked at Jackson, he could not really tell where to shoot. They are standing out and separated off.

If any of you know anything about dueling, you have a second. You have a man there with a gun, Jackson's man's gun is pointed at Dickinson and Dickinson's man is pointed at Jackson. If one of the two men cheat, they're able to shoot the other man. The two are paced off and ready to duel. Jackson is on one end, Dickinson is on the other. They raise their guns. Dickinson fires first and hits Jackson. Jackson fires and his gun misfires. Jackson is still standing. Under the laws of dueling, if your gun misfires, you are allowed another shot. Dickinson is absolutely in shock because when he raised his gun and fired, Jackson stood still. It appeared as though Dickinson had missed Jackson, which was completely out of character because he had shot every man he had ever dueled. At this point in time, he realized that Jackson's gun did not fire so Jackson gets to reload. Jackson reloads his gun, standing firm. Dickinson has to stand there and know that Jackson now gets time to fire. He has to stand there and wait for the shot. Jackson fixes his gun, he raises it with Dickinson just standing at the other end. He aims and mortally wounds Dickinson. Dickinson falls to the ground and within a very short time has died. Jackson by this time, who has been shot, the bullet actually hit him only an inch and a half from his heart, as he stands there, his second comes over to congratulate him and when he shakes Jackson's hand, Jackson almost collapses. There is blood running out of the top of Jackson's boot where he is bleeding profusely from his chest wound. They quickly put Jackson on his horse and take him to a nearby home. They call the surgeon. The surgeon is not able to remove the bullet in his chest because it is too close to his heart. Jackson actually carries the bullet for the remainder of his life. The bullet began to rub which caused infection in his lungs and thus leading to his death many years later.

One of the things that this did is that it set Jackson up as a man of principle and a man of his word. Even though to many people, especially in the East, when I say the East, I mean the New England States, they looked at Jackson as a rugged man, a rough man who fought in a duel. To the common man in Tennessee, it showed that he was a true man just like one of us. He was the common man. It truly led to people in your more rural areas loving Jackson.

That is one of the things that we see about Andrew Jackson even today. As we talk to Historians, you find that there are only two emotions that you feel about Andrew Jackson. You either love him, or you absolutely hate him. One of the things you will hear more than anything from modern historians is his involvement in Indian removal. Indian removal is one of the most tragic episodes of American history. When we look at Andrew Jackson, one of the things we have to remember is that we have to look at history through the eyes of the time that it was taking place. In the early 1800's and 1840's, we cannot look at Indian removal with our eyes of the twenty-first century. To do so is very unjust for Jackson because the will of the majority of the American people was for the Indians to be removed. For what reason did the people want the Indians removed elsewhere? It was simple. Every time we moved the Indians somewhere else, we always found gold. It was very much a political and a financial reason we were constantly moving the Native population. That is probably the one drawback in Jackson's era during his Presidency that we see going on.

In closing, as we talk about Jackson and his years previous to his presidency, the one thing that we have to admit about Andrew Jackson is that he was a man of principle. He was a man who carried out his Masonic virtues every day of his life. His affiliation with the Masonic Lodge was something that he felt very, very important in his life. He is one of only two Presidents of the United States who served as a Grand Master of a Grand Lodge, Harry Truman being the second and both Democrats. Jackson and his closest cohorts of friends had two commonalities with one another. One, they were all patriots. Two, they were almost all masons. His closest friend, Generals Sam Houston, and those people he surrounded himself with daily, were masons. It had a great influence upon his life and upon his presidency. To give you an idea of the type of man that he was, when he returned home from the presidency, he returned bankrupt. When he came back to the Hermitage, his adopted son, Andrew Junior, had squandered every penny that Jackson had made. The mansion and the plantation were in complete disrepair, and Jackson was ailing. He had lots of intestinal problems. He had heart issues. He had constant lung pleurisy. He was in very frail health, but between the time he had ended his presidency and the time that he expired this life, he had regained all of his wealth from the plantation. According to historians today, he died the wealthiest president in American history. This was a man who was able to do anything that he set his mind to. When he set his mind to something, it occurred regardless of what it took. That is a virtue that I am afraid all too often in today's society, we are lacking. He was a man of his word and a man of principle. Those are things that the Masonic Lodge fights to maintain in American Society.

THE TWO PILLARS

By: Joseph C. P. Kindoll

The first time that I ever got a good look at the inside of a Masonic lodge room was on the morning of my initiation. My grandfather took me into the lodge room at Carrollton (Kentucky) Lodge #134, and proceeded to inform me that everything in that room, down to the smallest item, was there for a very specific purpose, and that it all meant something—nothing was merely ornamental. My eyes were immediately drawn to the two large, free-standing pillars, which in that lodge were placed on either side of the entrance door. I asked him what they were and what they meant, and he replied, "Oh, you'll find out more about them later." That explanation did come a month later when I was passed to the degree of Fellowcraft.

However, in many ways the information communicated about these most important furnishings is not proportionate to their size and station. In Tennessee, for example, our attention is drawn only briefly to them in the second degree, and then the explanation is limited to their names, dimensions, and a description of their adornments. They are not mentioned again until they appear, almost as an after thought, in the Royal Arch degree, in the list of those treasures that were taken to Babylon by Nebuchadnezzar as the spoils of war. Little is given to explain the meaning or symbolism of the pillars themselves. In order to determine that, one must dig deeper into other sources, and that is what we will endeavor to do today.

These pillars, of course, are Masonic representations of those pillars that were erected in the building of King Solomon's temple. Scripture outlines the details of the temple, including the pillars, in great detail. These descriptions are included in both the book of Kings and Chronicles. 1 Kings, Chapter 7, Verses 15-22 tell us:

15 For he cast two pillars of brass, of eighteen cubits high apiece: and a line of twelve cubits did compass either of them about.
16 And he made two chapiters of molten brass, to set upon the tops of the pillars: the height of the one chapiter was five cubits, and the height of the other chapiter was five cubits:
17 And nets of checker work, and wreaths of chain work, for the chapiters which were upon the top of the pillars; seven for the one chapiter, and seven for the other chapiter.
18 And he made the pillars, and two rows round about upon the one network, to cover the chapiters that were upon the top, with pomegranates: and so did he for the other chapiter.
19 And the chapiters that were upon the top of the pillars were of lily work in the porch, four cubits.

20 *And the chapiters upon the two pillars had pomegranates also above, over against the belly which was by the network: and the pomegranates were two hundred in rows roundabout upon the other chapiter.*
21 *And he set up the pillars in the porch of the temple: and he set up the right pillar, and called the name thereof Jachin: and he set up the left pillar, and called the name there of Boaz.*
22 *And upon the top of the pillars was lily work: so was the work of the pillars finished.*

Most scholars hold that the pillars were not actually made of brass, as the process of making that alloy involves combining copper and zinc, which was unknown at this stage of history. Many contemporary sources that reference brass then are interpreted to mean copper or, more likely, bronze. I am told by W∴ Bro. Palmer that the pillars here in this lodge (Hiram #7, Franklin, TN), were carefully measured when they were made so that they would preserve the scale outlined in scripture and reflected in ritual.

2 Chronicles, Chapter 3 echoes much of this description, but states that "Also he made before the house two pillars of thirty and five cubits high, and the chapiter that was on the top of each of them was five cubits." There are essentially two explanations for the differing heights in the two books. One suggests that the overall height of each pillar was thirty-five cubits (18 cubits for the pillar itself, 5 for the chapiter, 4 for the lily-work, and an additional 8 for a base upon which the pillar was erected). The more commonly accepted rationalization is that, since 1 Kings indicates that the chapiter of each pillar covered one half cubit of the pillar's body, 17 ½ cubits of each pillar was visible. With both pillars taken together, their total visible height, not including the chapiters, is thirty-five cubits.

Whether these pillars were smooth or fluted is unknown, and they are commonly depicted in both ways. In either case, both Kings and Chronicles place these pillars on the porch of the temple, and therefore they are typically displayed as being free-standing, rather than supporting any portion of the building itself. Therefore, in order to enter the temple, one must of necessity pass between them, and I believe that it is this moment that we specifically refer to when we say that we are" passed" to the degree of Fellowcraft. For this is the moment when we pass from the profane world without and into the holy ground of the temple itself.

This notion of passing between two pillars into some holy space or higher realm is a common thread throughout antiquity. This is particularly evident with respect to the Pillars of Hercules, which stand on either side of the Strait of Gibraltar. On the north side is the Rock of Gibraltar, and its southern counterpart is either Monte Hacho or Jebel Musa (Mount Moses). Plato recorded the location of Atlantis as being beyond the Pillars of Hercules.

Renaissance depictions of the Pillars of Hercules sometimes include the phrase "ne plus ultra," indicating that nothing lies further beyond those gates. This phrase also can be interpreted to indicate the state of perfection that has on some occasions been applied to the craft of Freemasonry itself, more specifically to the perfect ashlar.

But while these naturally occurring "pillars" were interpreted as having a more symbolic, spiritual application, men have been erecting dual pillars in their sacred spaces since the dawn of history. The temple site known as Gobekli Tepe lies in southern Turkey, near the Syrian border. This hilltop site is the oldest man-made religious structure ever discovered, dating to about 9,000 BC (that's almost 7,000 years before the pyramids and Stonehenge). The ruins at this site clearly show that the temples there were circular structures, with two large free-standing pillars. These pillars are each capped by a rectangular block, which readily calls to mind the capitals described in the Solomonic pillars. They are also carved to take on certain human aspects, commonly believed to be the depiction of temple priests, who are wearing what appears to be [loincloths] or aprons.

The Phoenicians placed their westernmost temple to one of their deities, Melqart (who is nalogous to the Greek Hercules) just beyond the pillars in Cadiz. Their temples to Melqart, as with other deities that they worshiped, including Baal, Astarte, and Adon, all similarly were adorned with matching pillars located on either side of the entrance. In fact, it has been suggested that one of the primary reasons why King Solomon sought assistance from Hiram, King of Tyre and his master architect was due to the grandeur of the Tyrian temple to Baal. It is easy to see then how this notion of the pillars marking the entrance to a holy place was carried over from the Phoenicians to Solomon's temple.

But Solomon was erecting a temple to Yahweh, not to Baal or Astarte. And though the physical elements were virtually identical, they must of necessity hearken back to the Hebrew nation and their God. Mackey says:

It has been supposed that Solomon, in erecting these pillars, had reference to the pillar of cloud and the pillar of fire[,] which went before the Israelites in the wilderness, and that the right hand or South pillar represented the pillar of cloud, and the left hand or North pillar represented that of fire. Solomon did not simply erect them as ornaments to the Temple, but as memorials of God's repeated promises of support to his people of Israel.

This excerpt is included in the explanatory lecture of the second degree in some jurisdictions, though not in Tennessee. It refers to Exodus Chapter 13, verse 21, which states, "By day the Lord went ahead of them in a pillar of cloud to guide them on their way and by night in a pillar of fire to give them light, so that they could travel by day or night," after setting out from Succoth (which incidentally is also the name of one of the locations where the temple pillars were cast).

These pillars may also have had reference to the two antediluvian pillars of Enoch. In fact, the first Masonic mention of pillars is found in the Cooke Manuscript, dated circa 1410. Enoch, who was the great-grandfather of Noah, was close to God, and according to Jewish tradition, learned much important knowledge from God, including the arts and sciences and the laws of the universe. In order to preserve this knowledge, he and his sons (Methuselah, Elisha and Elimelech) erected two pillars, one of stone, and a hollow one cast in brass, and upon those pillars Enoch engraved his wisdom. These materials were chosen to protect this important knowledge against any future destruction by either "conflagration or inundation," as the stone pillar would survive a fire, while the hollow brass pillar would survive a flood. Evidence of this connection with the temple pillars, from a Masonic perspective, is still evident in our description of them, which includes a reference to their serving as vessels to preserve the archives of Masonry and to withstand "inundation and conflagration," despite the fact that conflagration would easily destroy two brazen pillars. And here again, we see that these pillars make reference to both fire and water/cloud, as they did in our prior historical application concerning the Exodus.

This recurring association of the two pillars with the opposing forces of water and fire lead us naturally to the most obvious of the symbolic expressions of these furnishings—that of duality. If we accept the association with the pillars of Exodus, one pillar becomes associated with water, and the other with fire—two equal, but opposing forces. The ancient symbol for water was a downward pointing triangle, while that of fire was the same triangle pointed upward. This clearly illustrates the opposing nature of these two columns, and is suggestive of one of the key spiritual concepts that is omnipresent throughout Freemasonry: "As above, so below." This same concept is repeated with equal force by the Masonic addition of the terrestrial and celestial spheres: "On earth as it is in Heaven." This also suggests the most tangible of all dualisms—the masculine and the feminine. The left pillar is named Boaz, which translates roughly to "in strength" and is clearly an active, masculine concept. The right pillar, Jachin, translates to "God will establish," is a more passive, creative notion, and can be directly associated with wisdom, or "Sophia," which is feminine.

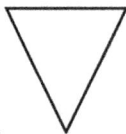

Dualism is an essential concept in virtually every system of religious or spiritual thought known to man. Whether this is expressed as creation vs. destruction; mind vs. body; or yin vs. yang, the notion of equal but opposing forces is omnipresent. Some depictions of the Solomonic pillars further reflect their oppositional nature by making one pillar in black and the other in white. This is NOT to be interpreted as equating to the notion of good vs. evil, for neither of these equal but opposite forces is inherently "better" than the other. We are told in scripture that there is a time to be born and a time to die, etc. illustrating that neither of the opposites is to be considered evil. Albert Pike further illuminates this distinction by stating that evil is not the opposite of good, but rather the absence of it, just as ignorance is the absence of wisdom and darkness is the absence of light. These dualistic forces that are symbolized by the two opposing pillars teach the concept of the necessary union of opposing forces, an idea which Bro. Ryan Driber names the "equilibrium of the contraries" in his paper of that name (Tennessee Lodge of Research 2005 Proceedings).

But a Masonic lodge is supported not only by the columns of Wisdom and Strength, but by that of Beauty as well. While these three columns are clearly delineated by the three[-]stationed officers, they are also reflected at one particular moment, when the candidate passes between the two pillars. At that time, there are in fact three pillars: the two we have been discussing and the third represented by the candidate himself. As he passes between them, he represents the harmony, or balance between the two opposing forces, between the Senior Warden's column of Strength and the Worshipful Master's column of Wisdom. He becomes the pillar of Beauty - the embodiment of the Junior Warden. Just as the union of the downward pointing triangle of water and the upward pointing triangle of fire yield the six-pointed star of Israel, so does the union of King Solomon and Hiram, King of Tyre yield the synthesis which is Grand Master Hiram Abif, whose deceased father was a Tyrian and whose mother was a "widow of the tribe of Naphtali." Much of the history and symbolism of Freemasonry comes from the Jewish tradition, and often more specifically from the Jewish mystical tradition known as Kabbalah. This school of thought teaches that God created the universe in ten utterances, each of which represents a specific attribute or emanation of the Deity. These emanations or sephiroth collectively form what is commonly called the Tree of Life, and are organized according to the three pillars of Wisdom, Strength and Beauty. The organization of these pillars exactly matches the placement of the two brazen pillars - Strength (Boaz) on the left, Wisdom (Jachin) on the right, and Beauty - often referred to as the Middle Pillar, represented by the candidate.

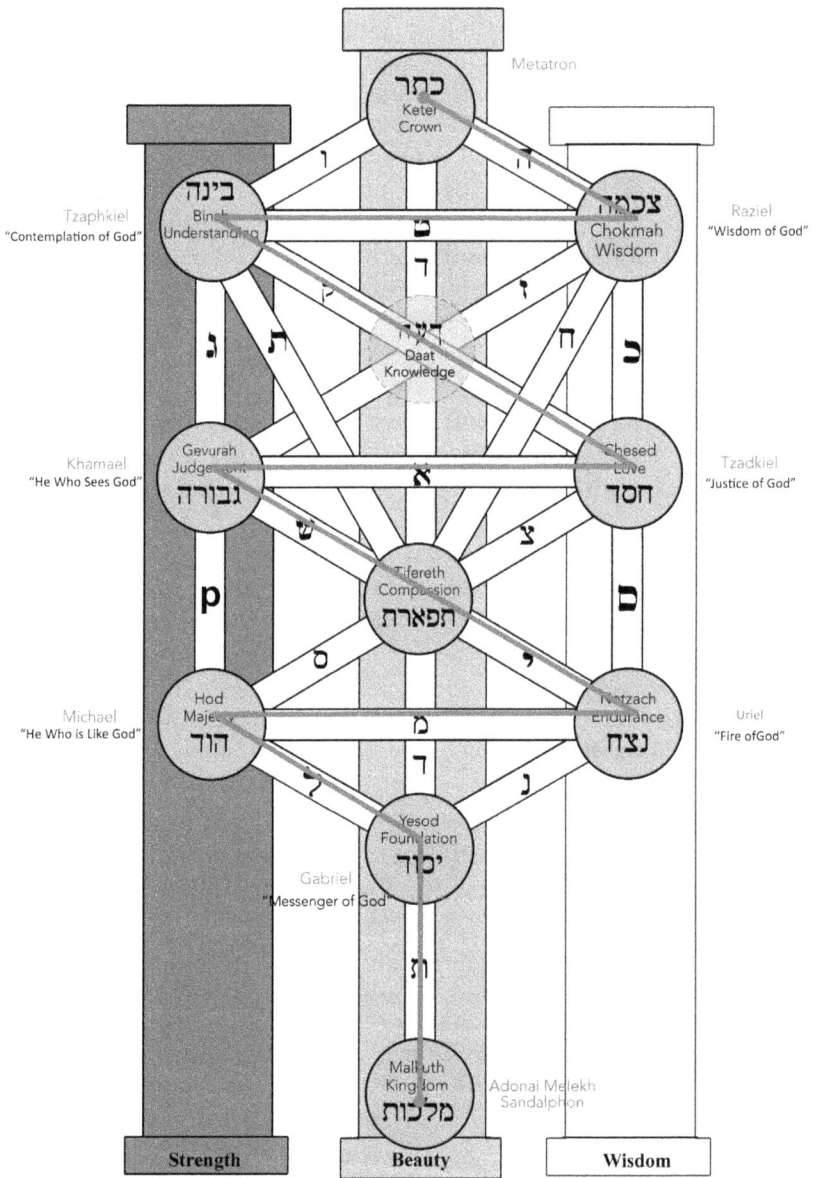

כתר
Keter
Crown

בינה
Binah
Understanding

צכמה
Chokmah
Wisdom

Tzaphkiel
"Contemplation of God"

Raziel
"Wisdom of God"

דעת
Daat
Knowledge

Gevurah
Judgement
גבורה

Chesed
Love
חסד

Khamael
"He Who Sees God"

Tzadkiel
"Justice of God"

Tifereth
Compassion
תפארת

Hod
Majesty
הוד

Natzach
Endurance
נצח

Michael
"He Who is Like God"

Uriel
"Fire ofGod"

Yesod
Foundation
יסוד

Gabriel
"Messenger of God"

Malkuth
Kingdom
מלכות

Adonai Melekh
Sandalphon

Strength

Beauty

Wisdom

The base of this Middle Pillar is the sephirah (Hebrew for a single emanation of Deity, as opposed to the plural sephiroth) named Malkuth, which represents the material world or kingdom that is generated from the other manifestations of Deity. It is the beginning of the Kabbalist's spiritual path toward enlightenment. The top of this Middle Pillar is the sephirah named Keter, which represents the crown or Godhead. In his journey toward the apex of this mountain of Truth, the seeker of light passes back and forth up a winding path between these pillars.

The goal of the student of this mystery school is to incline neither to the right, nor to the left, but to take from each pillar's energy, always returning to balance himself in the harmony of the Middle Pillar. The temple cannot stand without the two supporting pillars, and if the initiate fails to build his spiritual temple without harmony between the two extremes, his temple cannot stand, and will suffer the same fate as that which fell to Samson's might.

While the study of the Kabbalah is a deep and complex subject, even this cursory introduction shows a very clear parallel to the ascension of the candidate in the second degree. I do not claim to be an authority on the mysteries of the Kabbalah, or even on the symbols and meanings of Freemasonry. I do however believe Pike when he admonishes us to follow the streams of knowledge back to their "sources that well up in the remote past" where we will find the "origins and meaning of Masonry." What I have offered today is one interpretation of the history and symbols of these two omnipresent pillars. It is my hope that in doing so, each of you may be moved to explore these mysteries further, and in turn arrive at your own understanding of their meaning to you. My only charge is that, when you do arrive at a knowledge of this, or any other symbol of Freemasonry, that you do not stop there and say, "I understand this." Press onward, dig deeper, peel back yet another layer—for it is not the destination, but the journey through the pillars and up the winding staircase that yields the Mason his wages.

BOY SCOUTS AND MASONRY

By Jason F. Hicks

There is a deep and intentional relationship between Boy Scouts and the masonic fraternity. The Scout Oath and Scout Law should be seen as teachings within the masonic fraternity. The Scout Law is twelve attributes that every boy should strive for every day and they read:

A Scout is: *Trustworthy,*
Loyal,
Helpful,
Friendly,
Courteous,
Kind,
Obedient,
Cheerful,
Thrifty,
Brave,
Clean, and
Reverent. (1)

The oath requires its members to act as good citizens and men. It reads:

On my honor I will do my best
To do my duty to God and my country
And to obey the Scout Law;
To help other people at all times;
To keep myself physically strong;
Mentally awake, and morally straight. (2)

These are not merely meaningless lines - these same lines could be uttered by masons everywhere. From the very beginning of masonry, we see an undeniable relationship between both the founders of masonry and of Boy Scouts, and in how the organizations have developed through modern day.

Boy Scouts within America directly stems from its English counterpart, which was founded by Sir Robert Baden-Powell. Powell was a war hero from the Boer war in Africa. (3) He returned home to England in 1903 and found that his handbook which was written for soldiers was being used by youth all over the country to play the game of "scouting." Over the next couple of years, membership in the organization had tripled to 30,000 boys. (4)

The scouting movement had reached America with a number of different groups but none had been able to take off with the success that Baden-Powell was having. As legend has it:

W. D. Boyce was an American newspaper man and entrepreneur. According to legend, he was lost on a foggy street in London when an unknown Scout came to his aid, guiding him back to his destination. The boy then refused Boyce's tip, explaining that he was merely doing his duty as a Boy Scout. Immediately afterwards, Boyce met with General Robert Baden-Powell, who was the head of the Boy Scout Association at that time. Boyce returned to America, and, four months later, founded the Boy Scouts of America. (5)

Boyce was a Chicago newspaperman, and mason. He founded the boy scouts on February 8, 1910. President William Henry Taft agreed to be honorary President. (6) This tradition continues today as each and every President has been the Honorary President of the Boy Scouts of America. (7) The early days were a struggle and Boyce was loaning the organization $1,000 per month on the condition that it did not discriminate and any boy could join. (8)

There were other early scouting organizations that were in competition for boys across the country with the Boy Scouts of America. These were named the Woodcraft Indians founded by Ernest Thompson Seton and Sons of Daniel Boone founded by Daniel Carter Beard. (9) Seton ended up merging his organization with Boy Scouts of America in 1910 and became the first and only Chief Scout. (10) He served in this capacity from 1910–1915 when he resigned over clashes with Beard and James West. (11) There is no record that exists to say Seton was a mason. Daniel Carter Beard merged his organization with Boy Scouts of America in 1910, upon its founding. (12) He served as national scout commissioner for thirty years. (13) Beard was a mason in New York City and in Flushing, New York. (14) Beard went on to serve as the editor of Boys' Life magazine, which is still the official magazine of the Boy Scouts of America. (15)

From 1911 until 1943, James E. West served as Chief Scout Executive. (16) West's long tenure allowed the organization to flourish and his organization is what many attribute the group's long-term success to. (17) The group was competitive early with William Randolph Hearst's competing organization called the American Boy Scouts. (18) This organization was very similar, but more militaristic. (19) West sought a federal charter from Congress for boy scouts and was successful; it was granted on June 15, 1916. (20) West knew that by having a Congressional charter for boy scouts, they could shut other organizations down using the term "scout" and marketing their merchandise. (21) After he retired he was given the title "Chief Scout" which had previously only been given to Seton. (22) He was a mason in New York. (23)

Another masonic influence that can be seen is in the Order of the Arrow which is the National Honor Society of the Boy Scouts of America. (24) The organization started in 1915, at the summer camp for Philadelphia Council. (25) It was founded by Dr. E. Umer Goodman and Carroll Edson. (26) Edson was a Scottish Rite mason at the time, and eventually Goodman would become a Scottish Rite mason after the OA was founded. (27) The organization is set up in a similar way to the blue lodge, and has three honors. (28) The honors are ordeal, brotherhood and vigil. (29) According to one article:

In the OA, each honor has its own handshake, hailing sign, and "password." (For the Ordeal this is called the admonition. The Brotherhood member responds to a ritual question. The Vigil Honor has three watchwords.) Each honor has its own obligation and ceremony that intensifies the teachings of the Order. (30)

All masons will see an obvious similarity that ties these two organizations together.

The Federal Charter granted by Congress to the Boy Scouts of America on June 15, 1916, stated in part:

The Boy Scouts have not only demonstrated their worth to the nation, but have also materially contributed to a deeper appreciation by the American people of the higher conception of patriotism and good citizenship. Every nation depends for its future upon the proper training and development of its youth. The American boy must have the best training and discipline our great democracy can provide if America is to maintain her ideals, her standards, and her influence in the world. Anything that is done to increase the effectiveness of the Boy Scouts of America will be a genuine contribution to the welfare of the nation. (31)

The charter was amended in 1998 regarding certain provisions about Boy Scouts of America's trademarks. (32)

Numerous Presidents of the United States who were masons had a connection to the Boy Scouts of America. (33) President William Henry Taft was the first Honorary President of Scouting. Taft was a mason from Ohio.(34)

President Theodore Roosevelt was an active booster of the organization, and was a committeeman of a troop in Oyster Bay, New York. (35) He was also named the first council commissioner of Nassau County Council, was elected Vice President of the organization, and was the first and only man to be named Chief Scout Citizen. (36) Roosevelt was a mason in New York. (37)

President Franklin Roosevelt was the first president to have served as an active scout leader. (38) He served as president of the Greater New York council. (39) At his death, he had a twenty-four year service record with the Boy Scouts. (40) Roosevelt was a mason in New York. (41)

President Truman was a strong supporter of the Boy Scouts, and traveled to Valley Forge, Pennsylvania to open the second national scout Jamboree. (42) Truman was a mason in Missouri, serving as Grand Master of Missouri in 1941. (43)

President Gerald Ford was the first Eagle Scout to become Vice-President and President. (44) He is quoted as saying:

"One of the proudest moments of my life came in the court of honor when I was awarded the Eagle Scout badge. I still have that badge. It is a treasured possession. I am the first Eagle Scout vice president. The three great principles which Scouting provides—self-discipline, teamwork, and moral and patriotic values—are the basic building blocks of leadership. I applaud the Scouting program for continuing to emphasize them. I am confident that your ability to bring ideals, values, and leadership training to millions of our young people will help to bring about a new era—a time in which not only our republic will progress in peace and freedom, but a time in which the entire world shall be secure, and all its people free." (45)

President Ford was a mason in Michigan. (46) He was also a thirty-third degree Scottish rite mason. (47)

Today, there is still a deep and abiding connection between the two organizations. Lodges serve as charter organizations. (48) The Boy Scouts of America has a brochure that explains the process on how to become a charter organization, discussing the relationship between the two organizations, and how they compliment each other. (49)

There is an organization that brings masonic scouters together and is known as the National Association of Masonic Scouters. (50) The organization's purpose *"is to foster and develop support for the Boy Scouts of America by and among Freemasons while upholding the tenets of Freemasonry." (51)* The website even offers a page about recognition issues to make sure that no masonic scouters run afoul of their Grand Lodge. (52) The state of Connecticut has their own masonic scouters association which participates in Eagle Scout Court of Honors. (53) Each Eagle Scout is presented with a personalized commendation award and letter. (54) They also conduct an Entered Apprentice Degree at different Boy Scout Reservations. (55)

In 2010, at the Boy Scout National Jamboree meeting which occurred at Fort A.P. Hill, Virginia, there was a meeting of Masons in attendance. (56) The meeting was organized by the National Association of Masonic Scouters and hosted by Fredericksburg Lodge No. 4 of Virginia. (57)

James E. West's legacy lives on today, as in 1993, BSA created the James E. West Fellowship Award for individuals who contribute $1,000 or more in cash or securities to their local council endowment fund. (58)

The Pennsylvania Masonic Youth Foundation awards the Daniel Carter Beard Masonic Scouter Award to worthy masonic scouters. (59) The award criteria are based on both the nominee's masonic and scouting career. (60) As of December 31, 2015, there have been 2,746 masons that have received the award. (61)

In closing, the relationship between masonry and scouting is as strong as ever. The fraternal relationships of its leaders have been intertwined with the history of scouting.

Works Cited:

1) *http://www.scouting.org/Home/BoyScouts.aspx*
2) *Id.*
3) *http://www.scouting.org/home/cubscouts/parents/about/history. aspx.*
4) *Id.*
5) *https://en.wikipedia.org/wiki/History_of_the_Boy_Scouts_of_America.*
6) *http://www.scouting.org/About/FactSheets/presidents.aspx*
7) *Id.*
8) *https://en.wikipedia.org/wiki/William_D._Boyce.*
9) *https://en.wikipedia.org/wiki/History_of_the_Boy_Scouts_of_America.*
10) *https://en.wikipedia.org/wiki/Ernest_Thompson_Seton.*
11) *Id.*
12) *https://en.wikipedia.org/wiki/Daniel_Carter_Beard.*
13) *Id.*
14) *Id. and https://pmyf.org/programs/scouting/.*
15) *https://en.wikipedia.org/wiki/Daniel_Carter_Beard.*
16) *https://en.wikipedia.org/wiki/James_E._West_(Scouting).*
17) *Id.*
18) *https://en.wikipedia.org/wiki/American_Boy_Scouts.*
19) *Id.*
20) *Id. and https://en.wikipedia.org/wiki/James_E._West_(Scouting) (include copy in the appendix).*
21) *https://en.wikipedia.org/wiki/James_E._West (Scouting).*
22) *Id.*
23) *http://freemasoninformation.com/2010/09/bsa-100-origins-masonry-and-scouting/.*

24) *https://en.wikipedia.org/wiki/Order_of_the_Arrow.*
25) *Id.*
26) *Id.*
27) *Christopher Hodapp, Freemasons for Dummies (2005), page 249 and http://phoenixmasonry.org/freemasonry_soucting_and_the_order_of_the_arrow.htm.*
28) *Id.*
29) *Id. and https://en.wikipedia.org/wiki/Order_of_the_Arrow.*
30) *http://phoenixmasonry.org/freemasonry_soucting_and_the_order_of_the_arrow.htm.*
31) *http://www.scouting.org/About/FactSheets/presidents.aspx.*
32) *United States Code, Title 36, Chapter 309, Pub. L. 105-225, Aug. 12, 1998, 112 Stat. 1325.*
33) *http://www.scouting.org/About/FactSheets/presidents.aspx.*
34) *http://nationalheritagemuseum.typepad.com/library_and_archives/william-h-taft/*
35) *http://www.scouting.org/About/FactSheets/presidents.aspx.*
36) *Id.*
37) *http://www.masonicdictionary.com/presidents.html*
38) *http://www.scouting.org/About/FactSheets/presidents.aspx.*
39) *Id.*
40) *Id.*
41) *http://www.masonicdictionary.com/presidents.html*
42) *http://www.scouting.org/About/FactSheets/presidents.aspx.*
43) *https://www.trumanlibrary.org/places/gv36.htm*
44) *http://www.scouting.org/About/FactSheets/presidents.aspx.*
45) *Id.*
46) *http://www.masonicdictionary.com/presidents.html*
47) *Id.*
48) *http://www.nams-bsa.org/.*
49) *http://www.scouting.org/filestore/membership/pdf/03-294/03-294.pdf.*
50) *http://www.nams-bsa.org/.*
51) *Id.*
52) *http://www.nams-bsa.org/status.html.*
53) *"Connecticut Masonic Scouters Association", Emessay Notes, The Masonic Service Association of North America, Page 2, June, 2015.*
54) *Id.*
55) *Id.*
56) *https://scottishrite.org/about/media-publications/journal/article/current-interest-historic-meeting-of-masons-held-at-national-scout-jamboree/.*
57) *Id.*
58) *https://en.wikipedia.org/wiki/James_E._West_(Scouting).*
59) *https://pmyf.org/programs/scouting/.*
60) *Id.*
61) *Id.*

References:

http://www.scouting.org/Home/BoyScouts.aspx

http://www.scouting.org/home/cubscouts/parents/about/history.aspx

https://en.wikipedia.org/wiki/History_of_the_Boy_Scouts_of_America

https://en.wikipedia.org/wiki/William_D._Boyce

https://scottishrite.org/2010/12/jamboree/

https://en.wikipedia.org/wiki/Ernest_Thompson_Seton

https://en.wikipedia.org/wiki/James_E._West_(Scouting)

https://en.wikipedia.org/wiki/Daniel_Carter_Beard

https://en.wikipedia.org/wiki/Order_of_the_Arrow

https://en.wikipedia.org/wiki/E._Urner_Goodman

https://en.wikipedia.org/wiki/Carroll_A._Edson

http://www.nams-bsa.org/

http://www.scouting.org/About/FactSheets/presidents.aspx

http://www.scouting.org/filestore/pdf/210-211.pdf

https://pmyf.org/programs/scouting/

http://www.scouting.org/filestore/membership/pdf/03-294/03-294.pdf (flyer)

https://en.wikipedia.org/wiki/American_Boy_Scouts

http://freemasoninformation.com/2010/09/bsa-100-origins-masonry-and-scouting/

Hodapp, Christopher. Freemasons for Dummies. 1st ed., John Wiley and Sons, Inc., 2005.

http://phoenixmasonry.org/freemasonry_soucting_and_the_order_of_the_arrow.html

http://www.nams-bsa.org/status.html

"Connecticut Masonic Scouters Association," Emissary Notes, The Masonic Service Association of North America, Page 2, June, 2015.

https://scottishrite.org/about/media-publications/journal/article/current-interest-historic-meeting-of-masons-held-at-national-scout-jamboree/

http://freemasoninformation.com/2010/09/bsa-100-origins-masonry-and-scouting/

https://books.google.com/books?id=O7m29W5zShQC&pg =PA249&lpg=PA249&dq=carroll+edson+mason&source=bl &ots=2V_MdDqMMV&sig=7nV7VNVn6aNHtPx9_ca3bOqafs c&hl=en&sa=X&ved=0ahUKEwiKu6G4vJXQAhUV0IMKHVa-C3YQ6AEIIzAB#v=onepage&q=carroll%20edson%20mason&f=false

APPENDICES

ABOUT THE TENNESSEE LODGE OF RESEARCH

Purpose
Founded in 1985, the Tennessee Lodge of Research, F. & A. M. of Tennessee, is a subordinate lodge instituted to foster and expand knowledge of the history and philosophy of the craft by encouraging Masonic study and research, thereby assisting the Grand Lodge in its diffusion of Masonic light and education by publishing Masonic information and educational material.

Membership
All Master Masons who are members in good standing of subordinate lodges of the Grand Lodge of Tennessee, and all Master Masons who are members in good standing of any subordinate lodge of Grand Lodges of Free and Accepted Masons, or Ancient Free and Accepted Masons, recognized by the Grand Lodge of Tennessee, are eligible for membership in the Tennessee Lodge of Research.

Charities
The Tennessee Lodge of Research supports the Masonic Widows' and Orphans' Fund of Tennessee, the Grand Lodge Building Enhancement Fund, and the Grand Lodge Library and Historical Museum Fund.

Stated Meetings
The stated meetings of the Lodge of Research are held on the second Saturday of each March, June, September, and December in a dedicated hall in the state of Tennessee. All stated meetings begin at 12:00 noon, except as otherwise provided.

General
It is the desire of the Lodge of Research to encourage Master Masons to have more interest in Masonic enlightenment. Your curiosity in reading this information is an indication that you have a desire for more Masonic light. We, therefore, encourage you to request a petition for membership from your Lodge Secretary or from a member of the Tennessee Lodge of Research.

ORGANIZATIONAL HISTORY

At the Annual Communication of the Grand Lodge of Tennessee, F.& A.M. in 1977, M.W. Brother James Buck, Grand Master, proposed that Tennessee form a Lodge of Research. Although this proposal did not come to fruition at that time, it represented the first faltering step towards formation of this body.

In 1983, M.W. Brother John B. Arp, Jr., Grand Lecturer, former Director of Masonic Education, and well-known Masonic historian and speaker, was elected Grand Master. On April 13, 1983, he authorized Brother John Meldorf to inquire of the Grand Jurisdictions how to form and organize a Lodge of Research. Brother Meldorf contacted all 49 of the then-chartered Lodges of Research throughout the world and requested copies of their code, by-laws, publications, and any advice, both pro and con, as to the benefits and pitfalls of Lodges of Research.

After receiving a response from 31 of the 49 contacted, the information received was compiled and forwarded with a recommendation to the Grand Master in November, 1983. A proposed set of by-laws and changes in the Code was then forwarded to him in January, 1984. At the request of the Grand Master, the Grand Secretary, Brother John Stracener, prepared a proposed amendment to the Masonic Code to allow a Lodge of Research, which was approved by the Grand Lodge at its Annual Communication in March, 1984.

Following a notice to all Lodges from the Grand Secretary, an Organizational Meeting was held at Corinthian #414 in Nashville on June 9, 1984. By that time, 366 Master Masons from 92 subordinate Lodges had petitioned to form a Lodge of Research. With over 70 Masons in attendance, this meeting, chaired by Brother Arp, voted to request a Dispensation for Work, approved a set of by-laws, and elected Brother John Meldorf to serve as Worshipful Master under Dispensation. The remaining officers elected were: J.C. McCarley, S.W., Fritz G. Meyer, J.W., James Marshall, Treas., and M.D. Manning, Sec.

On July 31, 1984, M.W. Brother James McDaniel, Grand Master, issued the Lodge a Dispensation to Work. The Lodge first met under Dispensation on September 8, 1984, at the Lodge Hall of Hixson #727. It subsequently met at Hamblen #767 (Morristown), Angerona #168 (Memphis), and Cumberland #8 (Nashville).

On September 14, 1985, at Red Bank #717, M.W. Brother Sam Chandler, Grand Master, presented the Lodge its Charter pursuant to a vote of the Grand Lodge at its Annual Communication in March,1985. The Tennessee Lodge of Research has now grown to over 600 members from 132 Lodges in Tennessee and 5 from out-of-state.

Fellows of the Tennessee Lodge of Research 1985-2015

Name	*Date Awarded*
Howard Ketron "Jack" Akard	December 13, 1997
*John Burton Arp, Jr.	December 10, 1994
*Donald Barrow	December 10, 1994
Thomas Ernest Brooks	December 10, 1994
*Billie Reginald Brown	December 10, 1994
Ronald J. Coates	December 8, 2001
*Harold Cristil	December 10, 1994
Bobby Joe DeMott	December 10, 1994
*Jacob Roach Denny	December 10, 1994
Thomas James Driber, Ph.D.	December 13, 2008
*Charles Jahew Eads, Jr.	December 10, 1994
Robert Elmer Gooch	December 10, 1994
*Gary William Hall	December 13, 1997
*Virgil Marion Hileman	March 9, 1996
Dickie W. Johnson	December 9, 2000
Matthew Glenn Johnson	December 13, 2014
*Thomas Charles Kenner	December 13, 2003
Joseph Clayton Pryor Kindoll	December 11, 2010
*Billy Wilton King	December 12, 1998
George Caleb Ladd III	December 11, 2004
Sanford Dale Lancaster	December 13, 2008
Michael Carroll Lett	December 14, 2002
Moses Defriese Manning, Jr.	December 10, 1994
*James Allen Marshall	December 10, 1994
*James Clifton McCarley	December 10, 1994
John Russell Meldorf	December 10, 1994
Warren Lee Moore	December 10, 1994
John Lawrence Palmer	December 12, 2015
Philip Edward Phillips, Ph.D.	December 12, 2009
*Richard Travis Milton Prine	December 10, 1994
Paul Frederick Richards	December 11, 1999
Robert Harold Richards	December 10, 1994
John Nicholas Sharp	March 9, 1996

Fellows of the Tennessee Lodge of Research 1985-2015, cont.

Name	Date Awarded
Donald Martin Smith	December 10, 1994
David Edward Stafford, Ph.D.	December 11, 2010
*Louis Steinberg	December 10, 1994
Charles McBerry Thames	December 10, 2005
Vincent Lamar "Marty" Troglen	December 10, 2011
*Clarence Raymond Wilson, Jr.	December 12, 2015

Deceased

Past Masters of the Tennessee Lodge of Research

1985-1987	John Russell Meldorf
1988	James Clifton McCarley
1989	Robert Elmer Gooch
1990	Thomas Ernest Brooks
1991	Robert Harold Richards
1992	Warren Lee Moore
1993	Donald Barrow
1994	Donald Martin Smith
1995	John Nicholas Sharp
1996	Gary William Hall
1997	Howard Ketron Jack Akard
1998	Billy Wilton King
1999	Paul Frederick Richards
2000	Dickie Wayland Johnson
2001	Ronald Jasper Coates
2002	Michael Caroll Lett
2003	Tommy Charles Kenner
2004	George Caleb Ladd, III
2005	Charles McBerry Thames
2006	Ray Lee Covey
2007	William M. Williams
2008	Sanford D. Lancaster
2009	Marshall L. Horn
2010	Joseph C.P. Kindoll
2011	Vincent Lamar "Marty" Troglen
2012	David Philip Johnson
2013	David Edward Stafford, Ph.D.
2014	Matthew Glenn Johnson
2015	Clarence Raymond Wilson, Jr.

AUTHOR BIOGRAPHIES

Donald Edgar Brooks

Illustrious Brother and Reverend Donald Edgar Brooks was born into the home of the Reverend Weldon F. Brooks, a Baptist Minister, and Edna Mae (Taylor) Brooks, a nurse, in Alvin, TX, in 1946. Don completed High School in Woodlawn, Tennessee and later graduated from Austin Peay State University, Clarksville, Tennessee with a BA in English/Speech & Theater. He taught one year in the Clarksville-Montgomery County school system; then moved to Saulsbury, Tennessee, and taught school for ten years in the Hardeman County schools, leaving the classroom to become Director of Psychological Services. He earned his Masters in Education in clinical counseling and a Master of Arts in School Psychology from the University of Memphis.

He was ordained a Deacon, then an Episcopal Priest in 1982, later enrolling in St. Luke's Seminary, School of Theology, The University of the South at Sewanee, where he earned his Graduate Certificate in Anglican Studies. Father Brooks has served several congregations as Vicar or as Rector; as a special assistant and Pastor to the Bishop of West Tennessee, Examiner in Liturgical Theology, Homiletics and Canon Law for those seeking ordination in the Episcopal Church; Diocesan Program Director for Ministries in Small Congregations; and Diocesan Chaplain to the Order of The Daughters of the King, an order of sisters in the Episcopal Church. He is Director of the Emergency/Disaster Preparedness and Response for the Diocese, and has served as a Justice on the Church Ecclesiastical Court. Additionally, Brother Don has served as Chaplain to the Brownsville Police and Fire Departments, the Haywood County Sheriff's Department, and the Haywood County Emergency Management Agency. He moved to Union City, Tennessee, where he serves as Rector of St. James' Episcopal Church, Associate Chief Chaplain and Chaplain Training Officer for the Union City Police Department. He is a member of the Tennessee Public Safety Network Emergency Response and Debriefing Team, and served in this capacity with the Tennessee Team on the Gulf Coast following Hurricane Katrina. He is Vice President of the Obion County Ministers' Alliance. Don has assisted Temple Adas Israel, Brownsville, (the oldest continuously functioning Jewish Congregation in Tennessee) as part-time visiting Cantor, and has written and had published a comprehensive history of the Congregation and served as a tour guide for their historic building.

Brother Brooks was raised to the Sublime Degree of Master Mason in June, 1970 in Berlin Lodge, # 170, I & AM, Saulsbury, Tennessee. He served as Worshipful Master during 1976, becoming a plural member in 1998 of Ed

162

Worsham Lodge #505, Brownsville where he served as Worshipful Master in 2005. Don served the Grand Lodge of Tennessee as Grand Chaplain in 1996, and received appointment as Representative of the United Grand Lodge of England to the Grand Lodge of Tennessee in 1998. Active in the York Rite Bodies of Tennessee, Don received the distinction of Knight York Cross of Honour in Tennessee Priory #15 on March 27, 1979 and he has served as the Grand Chaplain/Grand Prelate in the Grand Chapter, the Grand Council, and Grand Commandery of Tennessee.

He served as Worthy Patron of both Ruth Chapter #35 and Haywood Chapter # 357, Order of the Eastern Star and is a member of Faith Court #15, Order of the Amaranth; The Royal Order of Scotland; Tralee Council #41, Knight Masons; West Tennessee College #141, York Rite Sovereign College and the recipient of the Grand York Rite College Service Award in 1998. Don is a Knight Companion of St. Stephen's Conclave, Red Cross of Constantine; Nicholas E. Oldham Council #378 Allied Masonic Degrees; Zaman Grotto, MOVPER and Al Chymia Shrine Temple; The Philalethes Society; the Scottish Rite Research Society; the Tennessee Lodge of Research, where he is a published author; Life Member of the West Tennessee DeMolay Alumni Association; recipient of the DeMolay Legion of Honor (HLOH) 2006; and is a former Rainbow Chapter Dad, and has been elected to membership in The Commemorative Order of St Thomas of Acon. Brother Brooks is a member of the Scottish Rite Bodies of the Valley of Memphis, Orient of Tennessee where he has served as Chaplain to the Bodies, and is a ritualist and member of the Director's Staff. He was decorated a Knight Commander of the Court of Honor in 1979 and coroneted as an Inspector General Honorary, 33° December 13, 1999, and in 2007 was appointed Chanter for the cast of the Thirty-third degree team. In the Grand Council, Cryptic Masons of Tennessee, Illustrious Brother Brooks was elected Grand Captain of the Guard in March of 2000 and progressing each year to be elected as Most Illustrious Grand Master on March 24, 2003.

Dr. Thomas J. Dribler

Brother Driber has earned a B.S. and M.S. degree in Healthcare Sciences, a P.A. In Medicine and a Ph.D. in alternative medical delivery. He is currently certified in HeartMath Interventions.

He was raised a Master Mason in 2001. He is a member of Hiram Lodge #7 F.&A.M. in Franklin, TN. He has served as Excellent High Priest of Corbitt-Doric Chapter and Franklin Chapter of RAM and, Illustrious Master of Franklin Council of Cryptic Masons. He has served as Grand Master of the Third Veil in the TN Grand Chapter of RAM as well.

Brother Driber has contributed extensively to the TLOR and served as Editor of Traveling East, a compilation of the first twenty years of The TLOR. He has published in multiple journals and Masonic publications. He was an invited Key Note Speaker for the Golden Trowel Award In Dallas, Texas and has presented Papers at numerous Masonic educational events. He is a Founder of the Nashville Scottish Rite Valley and TLOR sponsored annual Esoteric Symposium. He is also a Founder of The Society of Masonic Orators & Litterateurs, an invitational Masonic group of published writers and public speakers.
Brother Driber was coroneted a Thirty-third degree Scottish Rite Mason on December 2, 2017 and has serve the Rite as Co-Chairman and Chairman of the official Nashville Valley Study Club. He is the current Senior Warden of Moquedah Lodge of Perfection in Nashville, TN and has authored the Thirty-third degree manuscript entitled, Who Is Like God.

J. Rex Hartsfield

J. Rex Hartsfield became a Master Mason in Fidalgo Lodge #77, Free and Accepted Masons, in Anacortes, Washington in September, 1967 where he later served as Worshipful Master. He was also a member of Walter F. Meier Lodge of Research #281 and Grand Mound Historical Lodge #3 under the Grand Lodge of Free and Accepted Masons of Washington. He was also a member of Columbia Lodge #31, Free and Accepted Masons, and the Tennessee Lodge of Research under the Grand Lodge of Free and Accepted Masons of Tennessee. He was a life member of the York Rite Bodies in Anacortes, Washington and Anchorage, Alaska and a member in Columbia, Tennessee and is a past presiding officer of the Washington York Rite including serving as Grand Illustrious Master of Royal and Select Masters (Cryptic Rite) of Washington. He belongs to the Red Cross of Constantine, Allied Masonic Degrees, Knight Masons, is a past presiding officer in all of them and has served as Eminent Prior of Evergreen State Priory #41 of Knights of the York Cross of Honor. He is a charter member and Past Governor of Rainier York Rite College #54 and received the "Order of the Purple Cross' in 1992. He has also served as a Worthy Patron of the Order of Eastern Star and as Royal Patron of the. Order of Amaranth in both Washington and Tennessee as well as serving as Grand Royal Patron of the Grand Court of Tennessee, Order of the Amaranth. He is currently serving as Grand Historian of the Grand Council of Royal and Select Masters of Washington and as Chairman of the History Committee of The Convent General Knights of the York Cross of Honor.

He has been a contributor to The Tennessee Lodge of Research, the Maury County Historical Society Journal "Historic Maury" and has presented papers on the "Masonic Lodges of Maury County" and "The Contributions and Influence of the Family Polk." In compiling this history of Columbia Lodge #31 he has joined two of his major interest, those of history and Freemasonry. Brother Hartsfield passed away in 2013.

Jason F. Hicks

Jason was educated in the public schools of Putnam County. He attended The University of Tennessee, Knoxville graduating in July 2007 with a Bachelor of Arts Degree in Political Science (honors concentration) and a minor in English. He then attended Faulkner University, Jones School of Law in Montgomery, Alabama and graduated in December 2009 with a Juris Doctor degree.

Brother Hicks is an attorney and is licensed to practice law in the State of Tennessee and the federal courts of the Middle District of Tennessee. He is an attorney at the law firm of Moore, Rader, Fitzpatrick and York. He has handled cases all over the state of Tennessee. He has also served as an adjunct professor at Tennessee Technological University. Brother Hicks has been active in numerous civic organizations across the State of Tennessee. He has been active with the scouts as a commissioner and as a Scoutmaster serving the troop where he earned his eagle rank in 2003. He has served on the board of directors of the Habitat for Humanity. He has served as President of the Putnam County Bar Association and the Upper Cumberland Trial Lawyers Association. He has been on the board for the Tennessee Bar Association Young Lawyer's Division and is presently serving as Vice-President. He is also active with the American Bar Association. He is a member of Cookeville First United Methodist Church and has served as a Sunday school teacher, has served on the church council and as the lay delegate to annual conference. Brother Hicks has served the Tennessee Conference of the United Methodist Church as a member of the Board of Trustees.

Additionally, Brother Hicks is a member and the Master of the Tennessee Lodge of Research. He is also a member of the Dwight Smith Lodge of Research (Indiana) and the Pennsylvania Lodge of Research. He is also a life member of the Middle Tennessee Past Masters Association.

In the Grand Lodge of Tennessee, he served as a member and Chairman of the Masonic Jurisprudence Committee. He is one of three people who have been awarded the Masonic Light Award by the education committee. He has also earned the Bronze, Silver and Gold Volunteer Service Awards.

Companion Hicks was exalted in Cookeville Chapter No. 112 where he served as High Priest during 2013. Companion Hicks was greeted in Cookeville Council No. 112 where he served as Illustrious Master during 2013. Sir Knight Hicks was knighted in Cumberland Commandery No. 26 where he served as Commander in 2017. He is a member of the Grand Commanders Club in the Knight Templar Eye Foundation. Knight Hicks was inducted into Tennessee Priory No. 15 Knights of the York Cross of Honour on March 25, 2018.

Brother Hicks is a member of Cherokee College No. 152 of the York Rite Sovereign College of North America. He is presently serving as an officer. In 2019, he was awarded the Gold Award for his work within the Fraternity. He has completed the Companion Adept of the Temple Education program.

Brother Hicks received the Scottish Rite Degrees in Indianapolis, Indiana in 2010. He is a dual member of the Chattanooga Scottish Rite Bodies where he is presently serving as the Lieutenant of the Guard in the Council of Kadosh. He has completed Master Craftsman I, II, III and IV. He is presently working on the Haute Grates Academy through the Northern Jurisdiction and the College of the Consistory through the Guthrie Valley.

Brother Hicks is a member of George Cooper Conner Council No. 432 of the Allied Masonic Degrees in Chattanooga, Tennessee he is presently serving as Senior Warden and has been honored as a knight of the Red Branch of Eri. He has presented presentations at a number of AMD meetings and twice at the statewide AMD in-gathering.

He is a life member of the Knight Masons, member and Past Patron of the Cookeville Chapter of the Order of the Eastern Star, life member of the Middle Tennessee York Rite Association, member and past Secretary of the Tall Cedars of Lebanon. He is also a member and officer in the Masonic Order of Athlestan, Tennessee Court; he is a member of the Worshipful Society of Freemasons Rough Masons, Wallers, Slaters, Paviors, Plaisterers and Bricklayers; Ye Antiente Order of Corks; Grand College of Rites; the Masonic Order of the Bath; the first three degrees of the Order of the Scarlet Cord; and the Masonic Order of the 4 Black Lamas.

Joe Kindoll

Wor. Bro. Joe Kindoll is a Past Master of Conlegium Ritus Austeri No. 779 in Nashville, TN, and a member of Lexington Lodge No. 1 in Lexington, KY. He is an active member of the Scottish Rite, York Rite, Allied Masonic Degrees, S.R.I.C.F, and serves as a DeMolay advisor. Wor. Bro. Kindoll is a Past Master and Fellow of the Tennessee Lodge of Research. He has been published in Masonic journals at both the state and national levels, and regularly lectures at lodge education events in middle Tennessee.

James M. Kinslow

Served as Master of the Tennessee Lodge of Research, F. & A. M. Brother Kinslow was awarded a Master of Arts in Sociology from Middle Tennessee State University in 2012. His was a member of Mount Moriah Lodge in Murfreesboro, Tennessee.

George C. Ladd

Brother Ladd is Past Master, Fellow, and the current Secretary/Treasurer of the Tennessee Lodge of Research, having served in that capacity since 2006. In 2020 he was installed as Master of Kadosh of Trinity Consistory #2 in the Valley of Nashville, Orient of Tennessee of the Ancient and Accepted Scottish Rite, Southern Jurisdiction and has been coronated a thirty-third degree Scottish Rite Mason. He also currently serves as Grand Treasurer of the Grand York Rite Bodies of Tennessee.

Brother Ladd is a Past Master of Benton Lodge #111 in Santa Fe, TN, and currently serves the Lodge as Treasurer. He was raised a Master Mason in 2000.

Brother Ladd also pursues research as a member of the Allied Masonic Degrees and the Societas Rosicruciana in Civitatibus Foederatis. He is also a member of the Red Cross of Constantine, Knight Masons, and the York Rite College.

Brother Ladd is a retired software developer, having worked 26 years for the State of Tennessee Treasury Department. Brother Ladd is married to Rev. Sherry Whitaker Ladd, and is an Elder in the Swan Cumberland Presbyterian Church, located in Hickman County. He and Rev. Sherry resides in Santa Fe, TN.

John L. Palmer

John L. Palmer is a native Tennessean; he lives in Nolensville, Tennessee, with his wife, Glenda; and is retired from BellSouth Corporation and Electronic Data Systems. He holds a Masters Degree in Electrical Engineering from Tennessee Technological University and served as a Captain in the United States Army.

He served as the Grand Master of Masons in Tennessee in 1997 and as Grand Secretary from 2005 until 2007. He has served on the board of the George Washington National Masonic Memorial, as chairman of the Committee for Information and Recognition of the Conference of Grand Masters of North America, and on the steering committee for the Masonic Information Center of the Masonic Services Association. He is the Managing Editor of the Knight Templar magazine and teaches leadership seminars for the three national Grand York Rite bodies. He holds the honor of Knight York Grand Cross of Honor, the Knight of the Grand Cross of the Temple in the Grand Commandery, the Order of the Purple Cross in the York Rite College, and the 33rd Degree in the Ancient and Accepted Scottish Rite. He is currently serving as Secretary of Conlegium Ritus Austeri #779 in Nashville, Tennessee and as Chief Adept of the Societas Rosicruciana in Civitatibus Foederatis in Tennessee.

David E. Stafford

Wor. Bro. Stafford is a Past Master and charter member of Conlegium Ritus Austeri No.779 in Nashville, TN; a Past Master of Bethpage Lodge No.521 in Bethpage, TN; and a member of Trammel Lodge No.436 in Westmoreland, TN. He is a member of the Scottish Rite Valley of Nashville, all three York Rite Bodies, member and past contributor of the Scottish Rite Research Society, and Past Master and Fellow of the Tennessee Lodge of Research. He has a B.S. in Interdisciplinary Studies from Middle Tennessee State University, and a doctorate in Administration from Tennessee State University. He was a recipient of a 2005 Public School Administration Scholarship from the Supreme Council 33°, S.J. He has been published in numerous masonic periodicals including The Plumbline, Philalethes, The Knights Templar Magazine, and Ahiman: A Review of Masonic Culture and Tradition. He is a school administrator for the Sumner County Board of Education.